PAY LESS FOR COLLEGE

The Must-Have Guide to **Affording** Your Degree

Elizabeth Walter and **Debra Thro**

Pay Less for College: The Must-Have Guide to Affording Your Degree
2022 Edition
Written by Elizabeth Walter and Debra Thro

©2021 College Admissions HQ
https://collegeadmissionshq.org

All rights reserved. No portion of this book may be reproduced or transmitted in any form, electronic or mechanical, with the exception of worksheets found in Appendix A, and only for the express use of the reader. Contact College Admissions HQ at contact@collegeadmissionshq.org for any other permissions.

ISBN: 978-1-7356029-3-6

Contents

INTRODUCTION

Paying for College Shouldn't Be Harder than Going to College

College is really expensive and a great many students and parents struggle to pay for it.

There is a growing awareness that financial aid know-how is critical to avoid drowning in college costs. The problem is, the resulting conversation offers little in the way of "know-how," arming students and parents with only the most basic and ineffective tools with which to tackle this challenge.

The usual financial aid advice, "file the FAFSA," "use Net Price calculators," and "apply for scholarships," provides a false sense of confidence that this is all you need to know to get the best financial aid.

And every spring, when financial aid letters arrive, countless families are blindsided by the amount of money they must come up with. They *thought* they did all the right things—how could this have happened? This late in the game, with little recourse, many turn to unwise choices such as taking out large student loans, raiding a retirement fund, sucking equity out of their home, or, tragically, maxing out credit cards to pay for college.

What they needed was a *realistic* expectation of what any college of interest would cost them, *before* they even applied. This is a family's best defense.

People don't know what they don't know. And what those families didn't know about college financial aid cost them thousands, even tens of thousands of dollars. You don't have to be one of them.

Your Road to Success

Paying for college is difficult. But it's easy to wise up and confidently navigate a path that is consistent with your needs, resources, goals, and values.

- ✓ You can get a close estimate of what any college of interest will cost you before you even apply.
- ✓ You can save hundreds of dollars and a tremendous amount of time and effort in wasted application costs for colleges that won't give you the financial result you want.
- ✓ You can avoid painful surprises when financial aid packages arrive.
- ✓ You can save thousands, even tens of thousands of dollars in overall college costs.
- ✓ You can plan ahead for the college costs you will likely be responsible for at each college you apply to.

You can do this.

This Book Is Your Guide

The information and insights presented in this book offer true financial aid know-how and the power to save real money.

Chapters 1 and 2 boil down what you really need to know about college costs, Net Price, EFC, types of financial aid, and how to access aid.

Chapter 3 opens your eyes to the hard truth of how colleges build financial aid packages and what "meeting need" truly means.

Chapters 4, 5, and 6 help you discover sensible ways to seriously reduce the cost of your degree.

Chapter 7 guides families through a meaningful conversation to be sure everyone is on the same page about who is responsible to pay what college costs, and how and when those costs will be paid.

Chapter 8 prepares you for the many changes to the FAFSA and financial aid that will be phased in over the 2023-24 and 2024-25 school years. These changes are intended to make financial aid easier to access, increase funding to the neediest students, and allow more leeway for financial aid officers to adjust financial aid packages.

SEE CHAPTER EIGHT

Look for these signs within the text that will alert you to the coming FAFSA and financial aid changes. Refer to Chapter 8 for a full explanation of each change noted.

The five Appendices provide detailed supporting information and resources for those who want to dig a little deeper. They include Links and Resources, a Financial Aid Glossary, and thorough guides to the FAFSA, the CSS Profile, the EFC (Expected Family Contribution), and financial aid when parents are divorced, separated, unmarried, or remarried.

You've Come to the Right Place

Although the college financial aid system can feel intimidating, you *can* take control of it and we can help you. For ten years we have been dedicated to helping students and parents get the college admissions process right and achieve much better results. We are American School Counselor Association (ASCA) certified College Admissions Specialists, members of Pennsylvania Association for College Admission Counseling (PACAC), and founders of College Admissions HQ, https://collegeadmissionshq.org. Visit us online for more college admissions tools, resources, and information.

CHAPTER 1

WHAT YOU'LL PAY FOR COLLEGE

- The Cost of Attendance
- It's Your Net Price That Matters
- Net Price Begins with Your EFC
- Your EFC Determines Your Need
- The EFC Isn't All You'll Pay

The Cost of Attendance

The published sticker price to attend any college or university is called the Cost of Attendance, or COA.

The COA Includes Both Direct and Indirect Costs

Direct Costs	Indirect Costs
Costs that appear in your college bill	Costs that do not appear in your college bill
Includes tuition, fees, room, and board	An average of the costs of books, supplies, and personal expenses such as transportation, parking, extra food, laundry, entertainment, activities, etc.

© 2021 College Admissions HQ

SEE CHAPTER EIGHT

The COA will be expanded to include many more costs when the FAFSA changes.

On average, COAs are very different for different types of colleges as detailed in this table:

2021-2022 Total Annual COA for Full Time Students

Type of College	National Average	Range
2-year Public (in-state, non-boarding)	$8,300	$4,400 -- $11,200
4-year Public (in-state)	$25,600	$18,600 -- $34,600
4-year Public (out-of-state)	$39,700	$21,300 -- $62,900
4-year Private	$53,900	$21,600 -- $81,000

© 2021 College Admissions HQ

It's Your Net Price That Matters

Don't be fooled by the COA when shopping for colleges. COAs are sticker prices, and while you may end up paying the sticker price (especially at less expensive colleges), most students do not pay full price (especially at very expensive private colleges). It's your Net Price that really matters -- that is, the cost you actually pay to attend. Net Price includes what you pay now, and what you borrow and pay over time with interest.

Simply stated, your Net Price is the COA minus any free money (grants, scholarships, and discounts) you are awarded.

Your Net Price will be different at different schools because COAs are different. In addition, the amount of free money colleges award is both different between colleges and different between students attending the same college.

Net Price Begins with Your EFC

EFC, or Expected Family Contribution, is the *minimum* amount of money your family is expected to pay each year towards the COA.

EFC is determined each year by financial aid formulas that assess both parent and student income and assets. Most families are surprised by how large their EFCs are because they can't possibly pay that much money each year toward college. Unfortunately, the EFC is calculated to reflect not only what you can pay now, but also what you can borrow and pay over time. Borrowing to meet the EFC contributes heavily to overall student and parent education debt.

SEE CHAPTER EIGHT

The EFC information presented in this book is relevant for the 2022-23 school year. However, the EFC will be replaced with a new assessment formula when the FAFSA changes are phased in between the 2023-24 and 2024-25 school years.

EFC Determines Your Need

Colleges subtract your EFC from their COA to arrive at your Need.

COA – EFC = Need

Since colleges all have different COAs, your Need will differ at different colleges, and you may have Need at some schools and not others.

If your EFC is equal to or more than the COA, you have no financial Need at that school and you will be expected to pay the entire COA, unless you receive a scholarship either from the college or from an outside organization.

If your EFC is less than the COA, you have Need at that school.

The EFC Isn't All You'll Pay

Almost all colleges try to meet at least *some* of that Need with financial aid. However, the EFC is the *minimum* amount of money families are expected to contribute. Almost all colleges expect almost all students to pay *more* than their EFC.

There are only two circumstances in which you will pay less than your EFC:

1. You receive a scholarship that is larger than your financial Need at that school

   For example, if your EFC is $15,000 and the school costs $20,000, your Need is $5,000. But if you are awarded an $11,000 scholarship, you will only pay $9,000.

2. Your EFC is greater than the school's COA

   For example, if your EFC is $15,000 but the school only costs $14,000, you will only pay $14,000.

Chapter 4 explains some steps you can take that may help you reduce your EFC. Appendix D is a complete guide to EFC and thoroughly explains how your family's finances are evaluated in order to arrive at this number.

CHAPTER 2

WHAT IS FINANCIAL AID?

- Types of Financial Aid
- How to Access Need-Based Financial Aid
- How to Access Merit-Based Financial Aid
- Sources of Financial Aid
- Other Sources of Help with College Costs

Financial Aid is any money awarded from governments, colleges, or outside organizations, to help you pay the cost of attending college (COA).

Types of Financial Aid

Gift vs. Self-Help Aid

- Gift Aid is free money that does not have to be paid back. This includes grants, scholarships, and discounts.
- Self-Help Aid is money you can borrow from the government, or money you can earn through the Federal Work-Study employment program.

Need-Based vs. Merit-Based Aid

- Gift Aid can be awarded based on either your financial Need or your merit.
- Self-Help Aid is awarded based on your Need.

<table>
<tr><th colspan="3">Types of Financial Aid</th></tr>
<tr><td></td><td>Need-Based Aid
Meant to cover some (rarely all) of a student's financial need</td><td>Merit-Based Aid
Awarded based on academic, creative, or athletic abilities</td></tr>
<tr><td rowspan="2">Gift Aid
Does not have to be paid back</td><td>Grants
From federal and state governments or colleges themselves</td><td>Scholarships
From the colleges themselves or other civic or private organizations</td></tr>
<tr><td colspan="2">Tuition Discounts
Free money awarded to students the college wants to attract, but who do not qualify for their institutional grants or scholarships</td></tr>
<tr><td>Self-Help Aid
Must be paid back or earned</td><td>Student Loans
From federal and state governments
Work-Study
A federally funded on-campus student employment program</td><td></td></tr>
</table>

© 2021 College Admissions HQ

GOOD TO KNOW

Federal Direct Student Loans are a form of Self-Help Aid and are available to students with or without Need. However, students with Need will have more favorable loan terms (see below).

Private student loans and Parent PLUS loans are not Financial Aid but are sometimes deceptively included in a student's financial aid package.

How to Access Need-Based Financial Aid

Almost all colleges determine financial Need using the information provided in at least one or some combination of three different financial aid forms:

- The FAFSA (Free Application for Federal Student Aid)
- The CSS Profile (College Scholarship Service Profile)
- Institutional Forms (financial aid forms developed by the colleges themselves)

Each college will list clearly on their website which financial aid forms they require. To ensure that you are considered for financial aid where you apply, follow their instructions to the letter and never miss a deadline.

Many states use the FAFSA to determine eligibility for state aid, although some require additional forms.

The FAFSA

The FAFSA (Free Application for Federal Student Aid) is the primary financial aid form for need-based aid.

The FAFSA:

- Is administered by the federal government
- Is free to file
- Generates a SAR (Student Aid Report)
  A summary of your financial information sent to the colleges you designate
- Generates your EFC (Expected Family Contribution)
  The *minimum* amount of money your family is expected to contribute each year towards college costs

- Determines your eligibility for federal grants, federal loans, and Work-Study
- Is used by the college to determine the amount of college grant aid they will award you
- Is used by many states to determine your qualifications for state grant aid (some states require a separate form—see Appendix A for information)
- Is released annually on October 1
- Is required every year you are enrolled in college and want to access financial aid

Even if you think you won't qualify for need-based aid, you should still complete the FAFSA. Filing a FAFSA makes you eligible for Federal Direct Student Loans, even if you don't have Need. It also makes it much easier for a school to adjust your aid package if your financial situation changes during the school year.

For a complete guide to the FAFSA and how to file, see Appendix B.

GOOD TO KNOW

- You DO NOT have to file your FAFSA immediately after it is released each year. However, you *must* follow the deadlines of the colleges you apply to and your state's deadline. You should file *early* so you don't miss out on any aid you qualify for. But first, take action to be sure you qualify for the most aid possible.
- The information in Chapter 4 reveals what steps you may be able to take to reduce your EFC before you file the FAFSA.

The CSS Profile

The CSS Profile is a second financial aid form required by approximately 240 colleges and universities and some scholarship programs, usually in addition to the FAFSA. The CSS Profile:

- Is administered by the College Board and submitted under the student's College Board account
- Free if the student's family has an adjusted gross income less than $100,000, or if the student qualified for an SAT fee waiver, or if the student is an orphan or ward of the court under the age of 24. For all other students, the CSS Profile costs $25 for the first school, and $16 for each additional school

- Is usually required by the most expensive private colleges that offer very generous need-based grants
- Involves an exhaustive look at family finances
- Is released in October each year for students applying to college for the following academic year

For more information on the CSS Profile and how to file, see Appendix C.

GOOD TO KNOW

The CSS Profile delves deeply into family finances and takes into consideration both financial benefits and burdens not considered on the FAFSA. For this reason, the CSS Profile can generate an EFC that differs from the one determined by the FAFSA, which can work to the detriment of some students and to the benefit of others.

Institutional Forms

Some colleges use a third type of financial aid form, an Institutional Form created by the college itself, which is required in addition to the FAFSA. These colleges want more information about your finances than the FAFSA reveals, but do not want to use the CSS Profile. Typically, Institutional Forms are short and easy to fill out, asking only a few more questions about your finances than the FAFSA does.

GOOD TO KNOW

It can be difficult to figure out which parents must submit financial information when they are divorced, separated, unmarried, or remarried.

- The FAFSA definitions of marriage, divorce, and separation are not the same as legal definitions and the FAFSA definitions of "custodial parent" are not the same as those used for tax purposes.
- Reporting requirements can be murkier for the CSS Profile as it is dependent upon the requirements of the particular college.

It is critical to understand how these rules work to avoid the kinds of surprises that negatively impact your financial aid. For more information on who is required to report financial information, see Appendix E.

How to Access Merit-Based Financial Aid

Scholarships Awarded by the College

Each college posts its scholarship programs, the requirements, deadlines, and conditions for renewal on their website.

Some scholarships are awarded automatically—that is, every applicant is considered, and they require no separate application. Automatic scholarships usually are awarded on the basis of test scores, GPA, and class rank, but some schools award them for other specific or squishy factors.

Some scholarships are application-based – that is, they require an additional application and/or essay, portfolio, or audition. If you meet the qualifications, college scholarships can be well worth the time and effort it takes to apply as they may be significant awards for all four years of college.

Scholarships Awarded by Outside Organizations

Many outside organizations such as businesses, non-profits, and employers offer private scholarships to help with college costs. These awards always require their own applications and supplemental materials.

Links to reliable outside scholarship databases and organizations offering scholarships for military families can be found in Appendix A.

Sources of Financial Aid

Financial aid can come from federal and state governments, and from the colleges themselves. Almost all colleges will almost always award you the maximum you qualify for in federal and state grants and loans first, before considering how much of their own money they will give you.

Federal Aid

The federal government offers three kinds of aid: Grants, Loans, and Work-Study. You must file the FAFSA in order to be considered for any federal aid. Links to more information on all these programs can be found in Appendix A.

Federal Grants

Pell Grant

- All students who file the FAFSA are automatically considered for eligibility
- Available at all colleges that receive federal funds

- For students with high Need (EFCs below ~$5,850 for the 2021-22 school year)
- Available only to undergraduate students
- Available for a maximum of 12 semesters
- Amount of award depends on student's EFC and enrollment status (full or part-time)

  Generally, some money is awarded to students with family income below $60,000 but most of the money goes to students with family income below $30,000
- Guaranteed for all students who qualify and file the FAFSA on time
- 2021-22 maximum award is $6,495

  2022-23 maximum award information will be released in January 2022
- See the Pell Grant chart in Appendix A to find the amount you qualify for based on your EFC

SEE CHAPTER EIGHT

Pell Grant eligibility criteria will change significantly after the 2022-23 school year.

FSEOG (Federal Supplemental Educational Opportunity Grant)

- Not all colleges participate
- Awarded to students with exceptional financial need
- Pell Grant recipients are given priority
- Amount of award depends on student's Need (COA – EFC), how much other aid the student has received, and the availability of funds at the school
- The budget is fixed, and money is distributed on a first-come, first-served basis, so not all who qualify will receive a grant
- The maximum award is $4,000 per year

TEACH Grant (Teacher Education Assistance for College and Higher Education Grant)

Awarded to students attending a participating school and enrolled in a program designed to prepare them to teach in a high need field at the elementary or secondary level.

- Students must file a FAFSA *and* apply directly for the TEACH Grant through their school
- Student's must meet certain academic achievement requirements
- Students must agree to teach for four years (over an eight-year period) after graduation in a high-need field of education or in an area that services low-income families
- If a student fails to meet the teaching requirement, the TEACH Grants convert to Direct Unsubsidized Student Loans
- Maximum award is $4,000 per year

<u>IASG (Iraq/Afghanistan Service Grant)</u>

- Awarded to students whose parent or guardian was a member of the U.S. armed forces and died as a result of military service in Iraq or Afghanistan after 9/11
- Students must have been younger than 24 years old or enrolled at least part-time at a college or career school at the time of the parent or guardian's death
- Available for a maximum of 12 semesters
- Students do not have to establish need
- The IASG award is always equal to that year's maximum Pell Grant
- If an IASG-qualifying student also qualifies for a Federal Pell Grant, eligibility for the Pell Grant will be recalculated as if their Expected Family Contribution (EFC) were zero and they will receive the maximum Pell Grant. A student cannot get both the IASG and Pell grants.

<u>Financial Aid for Military Service</u>

- ROTC Scholarships (Reserve Officer Training Corp)

  More than 1,700 colleges and universities offer programs for training officers of the Armed Services (Army, Air Force, Navy, and Marines). Scholarships range from reduced to free tuition and a monthly stipend. After graduation, students agree to serve for a set number of years in military service, including active duty. ROTC scholarships are merit-based and very competitive.

- The U.S. Department of Veteran's Affairs offers varying levels of education and training benefits for those who have served and for their families.

- The following organizations offer scholarships and other financial aid for education: American Legion, AMVETS, Disabled American Veterans, Paralyzed Veterans of America, and Veterans of Foreign Wars.

  See Appendix A for links to these programs.

Federal Loans

Direct Student Loans

Available to all students who file the FAFSA. Almost all colleges award almost all students the maximum amount of Federal Direct Student Loans they qualify for. These fixed-rate education loans are issued in the student's name and do not require a co-signer. Direct Loans can be either Subsidized or Unsubsidized. You are not required to take them, but you are still responsible to pay the amount they cover.

Federal Direct Student Loans

Subsidized Direct Student Loans	Unsubsidized Direct Student Loans
For undergraduate students with financial need	Available to all students regardless of need
Government pays interest while student is in school	Interest accrues as soon as the loan is disbursed
Interest rate for 2021-2022: Fixed at 3.73%	
Origination fee of 1.057%	
Borrowing Limits for Dependent Undergraduate Students: Freshman year-- $5,500, $3,500 of which can be subsidized Sophomore year-- $6,500, $4,500 of which can be subsidized Junior year and beyond--$7,500, $5,500 of which can be subsidized Total borrowing limit for undergraduates is $31,000, $23,000 of which can be subsidized.	

© 2021 College Admissions HQ

PLUS Loans

Federal education loans in the student's biological, adoptive, and sometimes step-parent's name.

- An *optional* source of borrowing (should NOT be considered a financial aid award)
- Available each year to parents who do not have an adverse credit history and whose child has filed a FAFSA

- Parents can borrow up to the full cost of attendance minus any grant or scholarship money awarded to the student
- Interest rates for 2021-22 are fixed at 6.28% with a 4.228% origination fee

Federal Work-Study

This program provides part-time jobs arranged through the college to students with financial Need. Students are not required to take a Work-Study job or work the full hours awarded but are responsible for covering the amount of money a Work-Study job would have provided.

- Not all colleges participate
- Jobs are usually on-campus but can be off-campus at private non-profit or public agencies
- The amount of the award is based on the student's Need
- Pay rate is at least the current federal minimum wage or that state's minimum wage if it is higher, and students may earn more depending on the type of work and the skills required
- The typical award is between 7-10 hours a week of work, averaging $2,000/year
- The student is responsible for finding, applying for, and getting hired for the Work-Study job

GOOD TO KNOW

- One important feature of Work-Study employment is that wages earned do not get reported as student income on the FAFSA. This can be very helpful in keeping your EFC as low as possible. (More about how EFC is calculated and what you can do to reduce it can be found in Appendix D and Chapter 4.)
- You must earn Work-Study wages before receiving them. But your first bill will be due before you've had the opportunity to earn that money. Therefore, plan on paying your Work-Study award up front and using your wages to pay for personal expenses throughout the year.

State Aid

State awarded student financial aid varies widely but may include grants and/or loans to students who have established financial Need (see Appendix A for links to state aid). Generally speaking:

- Most states require that you attend college in your state or in a state with which your state has a reciprocity agreement
- Many states partner with the FAFSA to determine a student's eligibility for state aid, but some require a separate application
- State grant monies vary each year depending on the annual state budget, how many students apply for aid, and what the student's overall financial need is
- Colleges expect you to apply for any state grant money you are eligible for. If you do not apply, colleges will expect you to cover the costs that the state grant would have covered.

College Aid

Colleges themselves are usually the largest source of free money. Colleges award need-based grants and/or merit scholarships ranging from a few thousand dollars up to full tuition, depending on the school's financial aid policies and how desirable you are to them as a student. Colleges may also award "Tuition Discounts" to students they would like to attract but who don't qualify for need- or merit-based aid. These students may be children of alumni, students of the same religious affiliation as the college, full or nearly full-payers, or in some other way considered to be an asset to the incoming class and/or the college community.

College Grants

College Grants (free money) are awarded based largely on how the college balances three factors:

1. The student's Need
    - Determined through the required financial aid forms
2. How much the college wants the student to attend
    - Determined by how the student's application compares to those of previously accepted students and other current applicants

3. The college's individual financial aid policies
    - How much overall money the school has to award, how they like to distribute it (a little money to a larger group, or larger sums to a smaller group), and on average, what percentage of Need they try to meet

<u>College Scholarships</u>

College-awarded scholarships can either be automatic, based on a student's GPA and test scores, or may require a separate application. Those requiring applications are usually awarded for a student's academic, artistic, or athletic excellence, but they can also be awarded for diversity or for certain student attributes selected by a scholarship benefactor. College-awarded scholarships may come with conditions and requirements that are important to understand, such as maintaining a certain GPA or level of participation in a sport or arts program.

GOOD TO KNOW

Despite all the attention given to national scholarships, the colleges themselves are the most likely place you'll get any scholarship aid. In addition, unlike national scholarships, college-awarded scholarships are usually good for all four years of attendance.

Outside Scholarships

Local, state, and national organizations such as retailers, corporations, non-profits, churches, service groups, employers, businesses, and community institutions offer scholarships based on academic, athletic, or creative excellence, but they can also be related to religious affiliation, parent employment, or whimsical reasons like red hair or left-handedness. Usually, these awards are good only for one year.

Local scholarship competitions are frequently much easier to win than national or state-wide ones because the application pool is usually very small – sometimes only you! State and National Scholarships garner the most attention, but they are much harder to win. This is because the applicant pool can be very large--often thousands to tens of thousands of students. And these applications often require a great deal of extra work-- essays, portfolios, interviews, etc.

Links to reliable outside scholarship databases and military organizations offering scholarships can be found in Appendix A.

GOOD TO KNOW

Rather than spending countless hours hunting for outside scholarships and meeting their strenuous requirements, it's far better to spend any extra time you have trying to make yourself a more desirable college applicant. This will help get you a more generous need-based grant or lucrative scholarship from the college itself. Tips include:

- Keep your grades high throughout high school
- Take challenging courses
- Work on special projects
- Take on internships
- Enroll in one or two college classes in your junior and senior years
- Volunteer
- Get better at whatever you are good at

Other Sources of Help with College Costs

Tuition Benefits

A growing number of employers offer tuition benefits for both full- and part-time employees, and sometimes even their children. It's well worth it to find out if your current or potential employer offers a program to help with education costs.

Private Student Loans

Private Student loans are offered by banks, credit unions, and other lending institutions. Loans are in the student's name but almost always require a co-signer. Interest rates are usually variable and are based on the co-signer's credit score. Financial advisors urge students to take the maximum in Federal Direct Student loans before taking a private student loan because federal loans come with extensive borrower protections and payback options.

Parents should carefully compare the terms of any private education loan they consider co-signing to those of federal PLUS loans.

CHAPTER 3

THE TRUTH ABOUT FINANCIAL AID PACKAGES

- What Is "Meeting Need?"
- Mind the Gap
- How Colleges Build Financial Aid Packages
- It's the Net Price Over 4 Years that *Really* Matters

What Is "Meeting Need?"

All colleges start building your financial aid package by calculating your Need.

COA (Cost of Attendance) - EFC (Expected Family Contribution) = Need

3

SEE CHAPTER EIGHT

The EFC will be replaced with the Student Aid Index (SAI) when the FAFSA changes are phased in over the 2023-24 and 2024-25 school years. Colleges will continue to build financial aid packages as described below, simply substituting the SAI for the EFC.

If your EFC is equal to or more than the COA, you have no financial need at that school, and you will be expected to pay the entire COA unless you receive a scholarship from either the college or an outside organization.

If your EFC is less than the COA, you have Need at that school, and almost all colleges will try to meet at least some percentage of that Need with financial aid using one or more of the following sources of money:

- Money you borrow from the federal and state governments (federal and state education loans)
- Money you earn from the Federal Work-Study Program
- Free money given to you based on your Need (federal, state, and college grants)
- Free money given to you based on your achievements or talents (scholarships from the college or an outside organization)

Government awards will be roughly the same at all schools that participate in the programs, but they rarely are large enough to cover your full Need at most 4-year colleges. That leaves college-awarded scholarships and grants to make up the difference.

However:

Only 3% of all accredited 4-year colleges pledge to meet 100% of Need.

97% of accredited 4-year colleges meet less, usually much less, than 100% of Need, leaving you with a Gap in financial aid.

GOOD TO KNOW

- Scholarships are almost always used first to help meet your Need. Unless they are larger than your Need, scholarships from the college itself or from an outside organization hardly ever reduce your EFC or the amount in government loans and Work-Study you are awarded.
- Many colleges practice "Scholarship Displacement," a policy that replaces need-based grant money that you would have been awarded with scholarship money you earned through merit.

Mind the Gap

The Gap, the amount of Need not covered by financial aid, is usually the biggest surprise in a financial aid package and can be a significant part of your Net Price, the cost you must pay to attend college.

Net Price = EFC + Government Loans + Work-Study + Gap

However, you don't have to suffer Net Price shock when your financial aid awards arrive—with a few bits of information you can reasonably estimate the likely size of your Gap at any college of interest before you even apply.

How Colleges Build Financial Aid Packages

Online Net Price calculators are supposed to give you a fairly accurate, personalized assessment of what you will be expected to pay at any school. However, they often use old, inadequate, or sometimes even misleading information, which can provide unreliable estimates. And these calculators can't consider any of the squishy factors that may be part of the way a college awards its own grants and scholarships to reduce your Gap.

If you understand how colleges are likely to build your financial aid package, you can calculate a much more reliable estimate of what any individual college will cost you, which will help you better prepare to meet those costs.

Below is a step-by-step demonstration of how a fictional student, Emily, compares what her financial aid packages would look like at two different colleges. Use the *Estimate Your Net Price* worksheet in Appendix A to help you do these calculations for any college of interest to you.

STEP 1: Get Your EFC (Expected Family Contribution)

If you don't already know your EFC, you can get a very close estimate in two ways:

1. The quickest way is to use the Federal Government's Federal Student Aid Estimator, a simple, free, anonymous online EFC calculator. If you enter accurate income and asset information, the EFC generated will also be accurate. This link can be found in Appendix A.

2. Use the EFC Formula Guide worksheets in Appendix D to crunch the numbers and calculate your EFC yourself. This exercise allows you to look inside the EFC, understand how it is generated, and see if there is anything you can do to make it smaller.

Emily calculates that her EFC is $12,000.

STEP 2: Get Two College Statistics

1. The COA (Cost of Attendance) (found on the college's website)

2. The college's "Average Percent of Need Met"

   This statistic can be found in several places:

   a. <u>The Common Data Set (CDS)</u>

      The CDS is an online, uniform presentation of important data about the colleges that participate. Appendix A includes a helpful guide to finding and using the Common Data Set. Average Percent Need Met is found on Line H2i.

   b. <u>U.S.News Best Colleges website</u>

      Search for the college of interest on the U.S.News Best Colleges site. Click "Tuition and Financial Aid" tab of that college's page and scroll down to "Financial Aid." Average Percent Need Met is found in a graph depicting financial aid statistics. You do not have to join U.S.News or pay them for this information.

   c. <u>The college's admissions or financial aid office (call and ask)</u>

For demonstration purposes, assume Emily's schools of interest, College A and College B, both have COAs of $36,000. College A meets, on average, 91% of a student's need. College B meets, on average, 63% of a student's need.

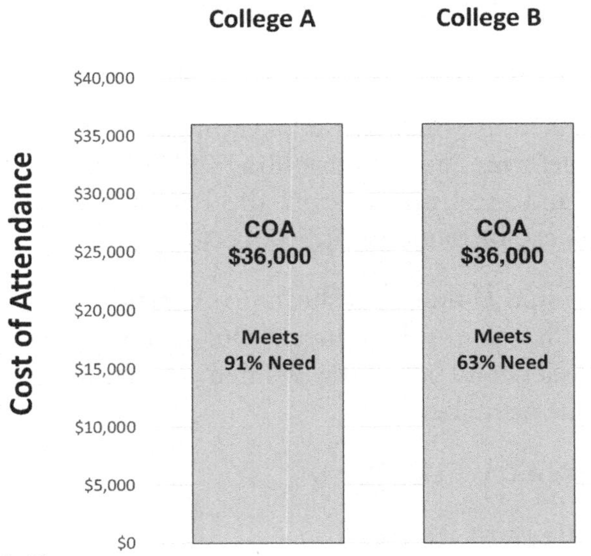

STEP 3: Calculate Need Using This Equation:

COA – EFC = Need

Emily calculates her Need at each school. Because the COAs are the same, her Need at both schools is the same -- $24,000.

<u>College A</u>

$36,000 – $12,000 = $24,000

<u>College B</u>

$36,000 - $12,000 = $24,000

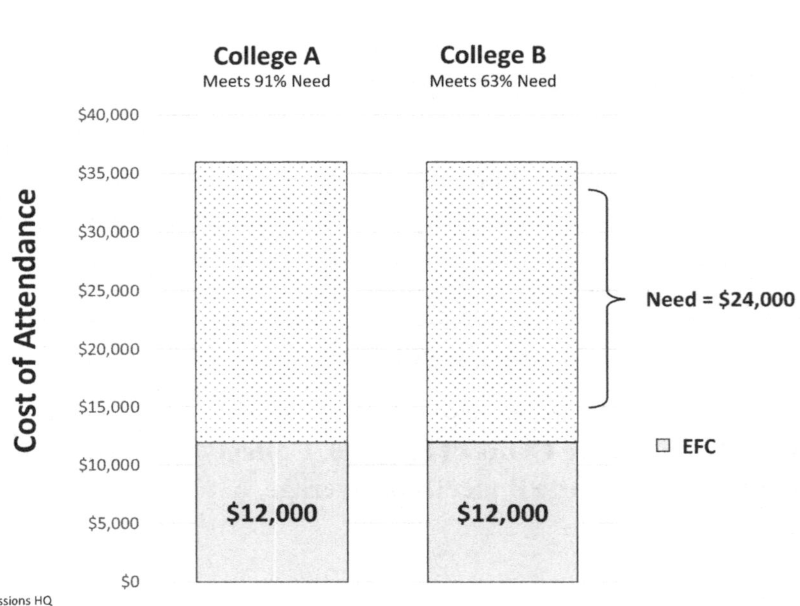

STEP 4: Calculate How Much of Your Need the College Will Meet

Assume you will receive the average percent need met.

Emily calculates how much of her Need is likely to be met at each school:

College A	College B
Meets, on average, 91% Need	Meets, on average, 63% of Need
0.91 x $24,000 = **$21,840**	0.63 x $24,000 = **$15,120**

The next steps follow the procedures most colleges use when building financial aid packages.

STEP 5: Apply Scholarships Towards Need

Almost all colleges will apply any scholarships you are awarded, whether from the college itself or from an outside organization, to your Need. This is disheartening because your EFC will not be reduced by any scholarship at any school unless that scholarship is *greater than your Need.*

It can be difficult to know for sure what college scholarships you might be awarded before you have even applied, but many colleges award at least some of their scholarship dollars based on hard data such as GPA and/or SAT scores. Check the college's website to see what scholarships you would likely qualify for and consider doing the calculations with and without the scholarship.

If you plan to apply for any outside scholarships, remember they are most likely to be good for just your freshman year—be sure you consider what might happen in subsequent years (See Chapter 5 for more details).

In our example, Emily qualifies for an automatic scholarship of $5,000 at both colleges based on her SAT scores. Each college uses this scholarship as the first step in meeting her Need.

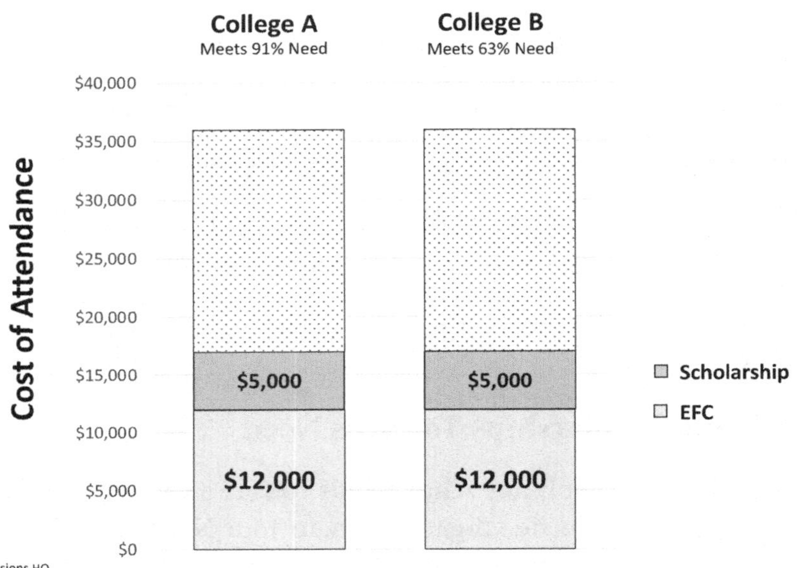

Step 6: Apply Government Grants to Need

If you qualify for any federal or state grants, the college will apply them next to your Need. See Appendix A for a chart to find the amount of Pell Grant you qualify for based on your EFC. See Chapter 2 for qualifications for FSEOG Grants, TEACH, and IASG Grants.

In our example, Emily's EFC of $12,000 is too high for her to qualify for a Federal Pell or FSEOG Grant, or likely any state grant. Nor does she qualify for Federal TEACH or IASG Grants.

Step 7: Apply Government Loans to Need

Almost all colleges will award you the maximum amount of freshman Federal Direct Student Loans, $5,500, and if available, any state loans you qualify for. (Some schools will apply scholarships towards reducing the amount of federal and state loans awarded, but the vast majority will not.)

Because she still has Need, Emily qualifies for $5,500 in Federal Direct Loans, which each college applies to her Need. Emily's state does not offer student loans.

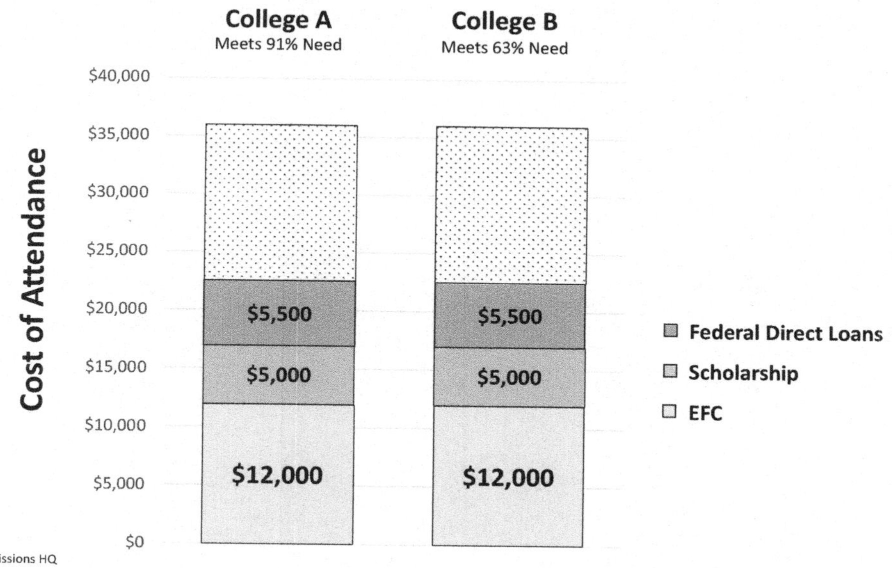

3

Step 8: Apply a Federal Work-Study Award to Need

If you still have Need, most colleges will also award you Work-Study, which averages $2,000 per year.

GOOD TO KNOW

- Students must earn Work-Study wages before receiving them. But your first bill will be due before you've had the opportunity to earn that money. Therefore, plan on paying your Work-Study award up front and using your earnings for personal expenses throughout the year.
- You are not obligated to accept federal or state loans or Work-Study awards. But either way, you are still responsible for the costs they cover.

Emily still has Need at both schools, and both award her $2,000 in Work-Study.

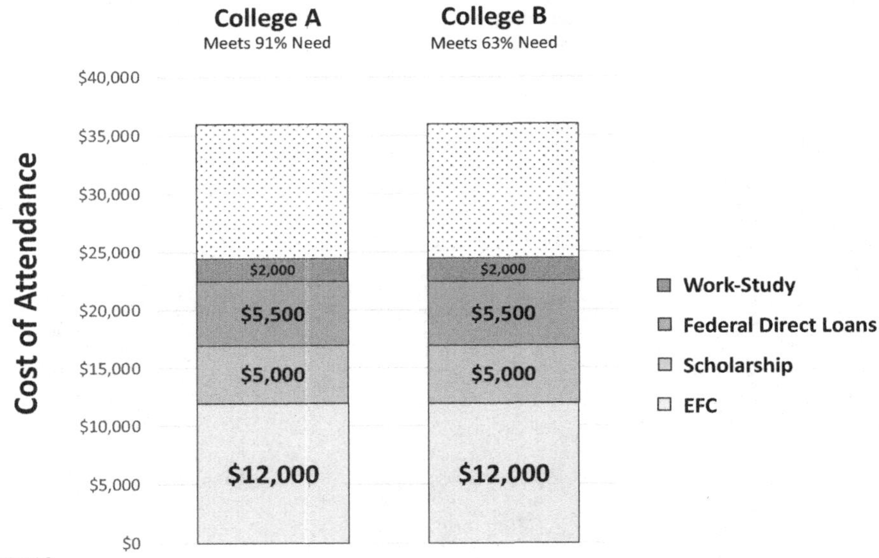

At this point in our example, the financial aid awarded to Emily by College A and B is the same.

Step 9: Apply College Grant Money to Need

This is where college financial aid packages can differ dramatically.

In her calculations, Emily assumes College A will meet 91% ($21,840) of her Need.

With her scholarship, Federal Direct Loans, and Work-Study, College A has already met $12,500 of her Need.

To bring their total Need-based award to $21,840, Emily calculates they will award her a $9,340 college grant (free money). This leaves a small Gap (unmet Need) of $2,160 that Emily is responsible for covering in addition to her EFC, student loans, and Work-Study.

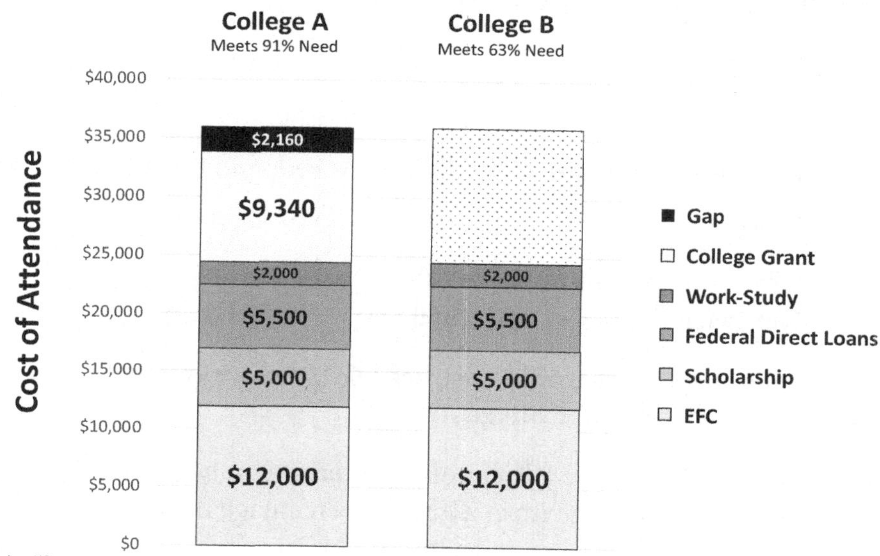

Emily assumes College B will meet 63% ($15,120) of her Need.

With her scholarship, Federal Direct Loans, and Work-Study, College B has already met $12,500 of her Need.

To bring their total Need-based award to $15,120, Emily calculates they will award her a $2,620 college grant (free money). This leaves a large Gap (unmet Need) of $8,880 that Emily is responsible for covering in addition to her EFC, student loans, and Work-Study award.

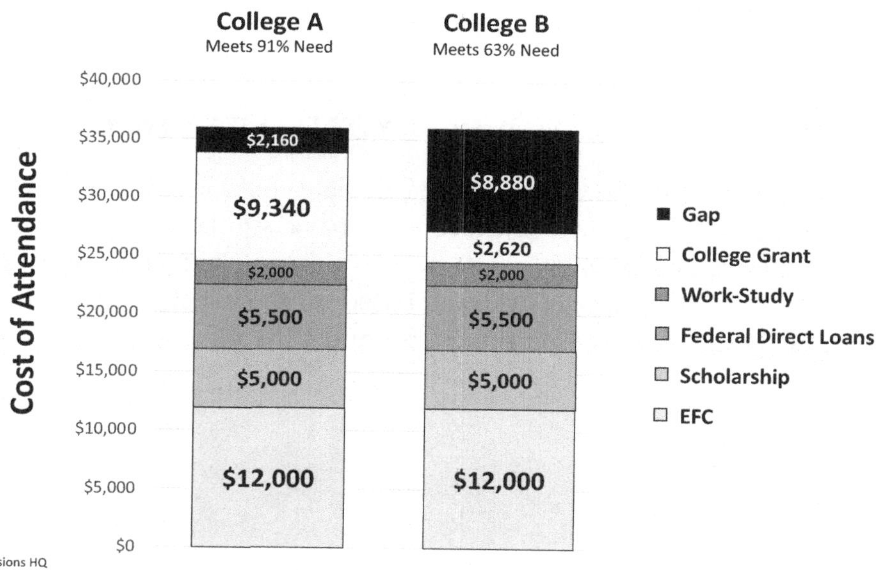

Step 10: Calculate Annual Net Price

College A		College B	
EFC	$12,000	EFC	$12,000
Federal Direct Loans	$5,500	Federal Direct Loans	$5,500
Work-Study	$2,000	Work-Study	$2,000
Gap	$2,160	Gap	$8,880
Net Price	**$21,660**	**Net Price**	**$28,380**

Emily estimates that it would cost her $6,720 more in her first year to attend College B than to attend College A.

Doing this calculation for all schools of interest can help you identify and apply to schools that, on average meet a greater percentage of a student's need and will leave you with a smaller Gap and a lower Net Price.

GOOD TO KNOW

This method uses the ***average*** percent of need met to determine the size of the college grant you will receive. Not everyone receives the average – you could receive considerably more or considerably less, depending on how much the college wants you to attend. Chapter 4 offers tips on how to improve your chances of landing bigger bucks.

It's the Net Price Over 4 Years That *Really* Matters

This demonstration shows you how to calculate your likely Net Price at any college for your first year. You will be expected to pay a similar amount for four years at some colleges, and possibly a lot more at others. Chapter 5 shows you how to calculate your likely 4-year price tag based on the college's financial aid policies and how they award funds in the 2nd, 3rd, and 4th years.

GOOD TO KNOW

Once you have done this calculation for each college of interest, you may consider dropping some from your list to avoid applying to schools you can reasonably assume will cost you more than you can or want to pay for college.

But before you give up on a college, consider the strategies offered in the next chapter that can help reduce Net Price. The first set of strategies addresses ways to minimize your EFC and increase your Need. The second set of strategies addresses how you can influence the wild card in your financial aid package – the size of the college's free money awards (grants and scholarships).

CHAPTER 4

HOW TO REDUCE YOUR NET PRICE

- Minimize Your EFC
- Maximize Your Free Money

It's not the college sticker prices but your Net Price, the amount you will actually pay to attend college, that matters. This includes what you pay now, and what you borrow and will pay over time, with interest.

Your Net Price is the COA (Cost of Attendance) minus any free money (grants, scholarships, and discounts) you are awarded. As illustrated in Chapter 3's demonstration of how colleges build financial aid packages, there are really only two ways to get more free money:

Minimize Your EFC
and/or
Maximize the Amount of Free Money You Get From the College Itself

Minimize Your EFC

SEE CHAPTER EIGHT

EFC information presented below is relevant for the 2022-23 school year. However, the EFC will be replaced with a new assessment formula when the FAFSA changes are phased in over the 2023-24 and 2024-25 school years.

Your EFC (Expected Family Contribution) forms the base of all your financial aid packages and is the *minimum* dollar amount your family is expected to pay for college each year.

You will pay *less* than your EFC only if:

- Your EFC is greater than the college's COA, or
- You receive merit aid (scholarship) that is larger than your financial Need

Most students must pay *more* than their EFC each year.

Your EFC is generated annually from the financial information you report on the FAFSA, sometimes in conjunction with additional forms. (More information can be found in Chapter 2 and Appendices B, C, and D.)

Colleges use your EFC to determine your financial Need at their school using this simple equation:

COA – Your EFC = Your Need

If your EFC is less than the college's COA, you qualify for need-based financial aid, including federal and state grants and loans, and Federal Work-Study. Depending on a college's financial aid policies and how much they want you to attend, colleges can add some of their own money (grants, scholarships, and discounts) in order to meet more of your financial Need.

The lower your EFC, the more need-based aid you can get.

The most important things you need to know about EFC can be organized into 3 buckets:

- Seven EFC Facts
- The Four Biggest Factors That Affect the Size of Your EFC
- Strategies That May Reduce EFC

Seven EFC Facts

FACT #1 – Parents of dependent students are required to report financial information on the FAFSA. "Dependency" in college financial aid isn't the same as dependency for tax purposes. To be considered independent, a student must be at least one of the following:

- 24 years old or older
- Married (or separated, but not divorced)
- A graduate or professional student
- Providing more than half the financial support for a dependent child(ren) or other dependents
- An orphan, in foster care, or a ward of the court
- In legal guardianship or an emancipated minor
- Homeless (or at risk of being homeless)
- Currently serving in the Armed Forces or a veteran of the Armed Forces

FACT #2-- Parents and dependent students *each* have a contribution to the EFC based on different assessments of their income and assets.

Parent Contribution:

4% - 26% parent adjusted gross income

plus

2.6% - 5.6% parent assets (after a small asset protection allowance based on the older parent's age)

Student Contribution:

50% of student taxed and untaxed income over a fixed annual income protection allowance of $7,040 (for 2022-23)

plus

20% of student assets (no asset protection allowance)

FACT #3 -- Parents have only one contribution to the EFC, which is split between siblings who attend college at the same time.

FACT #4 -- The income you report (both student and parent, taxed and untaxed) is from prior-prior year; for example, if you are entering college in fall of 2022, you are required to report income from 2020.

FACT #5 -- The net value of both parent and student assets is reported *as of the day* you file the FAFSA (see Appendix B for a list of all reportable and excluded assets).

FACT #6 -- Student income includes untaxed cash gifts and bills paid on the student's behalf by anyone other than the custodial parents.

FACT #7 -- The EFC formula does not take into consideration your cost of living (except for a small allowance based on the state in which you live), your consumer debt, any other college debt, mortgage payments, or other debt. (However, special financial circumstances, such as high medical debt, sudden loss of wages, variable income year-to-year, and other financial burdens, should be discussed with each college's financial aid office. While not guaranteed, colleges may consider these special circumstances and adjust your EFC accordingly.)

The Four Biggest Factors That Affect the Size of Your EFC

Factor #1: Parent Income

Parent income usually has the greatest impact on the EFC.

The table below shows calculations based on parent Adjusted Gross Income alone. The actual EFC will likely be even larger when parent assets and student income and assets are included.

Effect of Parent Income on EFC		
TOTAL PARENT INCOME	% OF PARENT INCOME	CONTRIBUTION TO EFC FROM PARENT INCOME
$25,000	0	-$750
$50,000	4.5%	$2,200
$75,000	10.4%	$7,800
$100,000	16.4%	$16,400
$125,000	19.5%	$24,400
$150,000	21.5%	$32,200
$175,000	22.9%	$40,000
$200,000	23.9%	$47,800
$225,000	24.6%	$55,300
$250,000	25.2%	$62,900
$275,000	25.6%	$70,500
$300,000	26.0%	$78,000
Calculations do not include parent assets or student income and assets and are based on a family of 4 (2 parents, 2 children), both parents working, equal parent salaries, one child attending college.		

© 2021 College Admissions HQ

Factor #2: The Number of Children Enrolled at the Same Time

Having more than one child attending college at the same time can have a significant impact on EFC because even though each *child* might have a different contribution from his or her own income or assets, the *parent* contribution to the EFC is split among those children.

Calculated Parent Contribution to EFC	Number of Children in College	Parent Contribution to Each Child's EFC	Total parent Contribution
$8,000	1	$8,000	$8,000
	2	$4,000	
$14,000	1	$14,000	$14,000
	2	$7,000	
$20,000	1	$20,000	$20,000
	2	$10,000	
$30,000	1	$30,000	$30,000
	2	$15,000	

© 2021 College Admissions HQ

In addition to a large savings for the family in terms of the total parent contribution, each student's EFC will be significantly less if a sibling is also in college, making them both eligible for more financial aid.

Factor #3: Student Income Above the Annual Income Protection Allowance

The 2022-23 student income protection allowance (IPA) is $7,040. After subtracting tax allowances and the IPA, 50% of any income (taxed and untaxed) above the income protection allowance is added to the EFC. This calculation hurts industrious students who work many hours and earn more than ~$7,040 each year. It also hurts students who receive large cash gifts or financial help with any bills (including college bills) from relatives or anyone other than a parent, since that will be assessed as untaxed student income.

GOOD TO KNOW

Wages earned in college through the Federal Work-Study program are not counted in the EFC formula.

Factor #4: Student Assets

Student Assets include savings and checking balances; the current value (not face value) of savings bonds *owned* by the student (not of which he/she is the beneficiary); and other investments as outlined in Appendix B, as of the day you file the FAFSA. They are assessed at a straight 20% with *no asset protection allowance.*

GOOD TO KNOW

Unspent student income from prior-prior year that is saved in a student's checking or savings account will be assessed twice – as income *and* as an asset. For example:

- Every $1,000 of taxed or untaxed prior-prior year income *less than* the income protection allowance that is unspent the day you file the FAFSA will only be assessed as an asset at 20% and will raise the EFC by $200.
- However, every $1,000 of taxed or untaxed prior-prior year income *greater than* the income protection allowance that is unspent the day you file the FAFSA will raise the EFC by $700 because it will be assessed as student income at 50% *and* as a student asset at 20%.

Strategies That May Reduce Your EFC

The ideas presented in this section are for your consideration and are not meant to serve as financial advice. Every family's financial situation is unique. You should thoroughly crunch numbers and/or speak with a financial consultant before making decisions about whether any of these strategies will work to your benefit.

The following strategies are divided into those that target income and those that target assets.

Strategies Targeting Income:

It's "prior-prior" year income that is assessed, so the following three strategies targeting income should be considered from the spring of the student's high school sophomore year through the end of the first semester of the student's college sophomore year (see table below).

College Year	FAFSA Form	FAFSA Form Release Date	Income Year
2022-23	2022-23	Oct 1, 2021	2020 –spring HS sophomore/fall HS junior
2023-24	2023-24	Oct 1, 2022	2021 –spring HS junior/fall HS senior
2024-25	2024-25	Oct 1, 2023	2022—spring HS senior/ fall college freshman
2025-26	2025-26	Oct 1, 2024	2023—spring college freshman/fall college sophomore

© 2021 College Admissions HQ

- **Avoid capital gains.**

  Capital gains are income -- Avoid selling property or cashing in stocks or offset capital gains with capital losses.

- **Keep student income under $7,040.**

  The 2022-23 FAFSA student income protection allowance (for 2020 income) is $7,040.

GOOD TO KNOW

Rather than trying to make as much money as possible in high school, consider working fewer hours and using the extra time to make yourself a more desirable college applicant. This includes:

- Keep your grades high throughout high school
- Take challenging courses
- Work on special projects
- Take on internships
- Enroll in one or two college classes
- Volunteer
- Get better at whatever you are good at

These activities can add up to more merit or need-based aid. Even small increases in GPA or test scores can result in your getting many thousands of dollars more in scholarships or grants than you could have made working at a part-time job in high school.

- **Establish Independence before filing the FAFSA.**

  Independent students do not have to report parent finances, usually resulting in a much smaller EFC. Most students can't become independent as defined by the FAFSA until they are 24; but if you planned on getting married or joining the military anyway, and do so before filing the FAFSA, you will be considered an independent student.

The next three strategies targeting income apply to the 2022-23 FAFSA which is set to change in 2023-24 or 2024-25 (see Chapter 8).

- **Ask grandparents or others who want to give the student cash gifts to wait.**

  In the 2022-23 FAFSA, cash gifts to the student in 2020 are considered untaxed student income. If a student has made more than $7,040 in total income in 2020, cash gifts in 2020 will raise the EFC by half the value of the gift. This may hold true for the 2023-24 FAFSA (2021 income) depending on when the FAFSA changes are fully implemented.

  Consider whether it's better to wait to give large cash gifts to a student until 2022 and beyond. Gifts should be spent (either for current college expenses or to pay down student loans) before filing the next year's FAFSA to avoid having them count as assets.

GOOD TO KNOW

Cash gifts to *parents* are not reported on the FAFSA. Grandparents or others can gift money to the parents, who may use it toward college costs. To avoid having it count as a parent asset, it should be spent before filing the FAFSA.

However, currently, and likely even after the new FAFSA changes are in place, Grandparent 529s and cash gifts to parents or students must be reported on the CSS Profile and possibly some Institutional forms.

- **Don't let anyone except parents pay tuition or any other expenses on the student's behalf.**

  In the 2022-23 FAFSA, direct payments or money given to the student by anyone other than the custodial parent(s) in 2020 for tuition, room and board, rent, car payments, medical bills, tutoring, lessons, etc., will be counted as untaxed student income.

  Although the existence of 529s in a grandparent's name is not reported on the FAFSA, any 2020 *distributions* from that 529 count as student untaxed income on the 2022-23 FAFSA and, if they exceed the student income allowance, will be assessed at 50%.

  Consider that this may hold true for the 2023-24 FAFSA (2021 income) depending on when the FAFSA changes are fully implemented.

SEE CHAPTER EIGHT

Most untaxed student income will no longer be reported when the FAFSA changes.

- **If parents are divorced, a student should live with the parent with the lower income for more than six months per year.**

  For the 2022-23 FAFSA, only the parent you live with for the majority of the year is required to provide financial information on the FAFSA, so your EFC will not reflect the noncustodial parent's income. However, if the parent with lower income is remarried, the step-parent will be required to report income and assets on the FAFSA, which may not work to your advantage. (See Appendix E for more information.)

SEE CHAPTER EIGHT

The parent who is required to report income and assets will change when the FAFSA changes.

GOOD TO KNOW

The CSS Profile and some Institutional forms require both noncustodial parent and step-parent financial information.

Strategies Targeting Assets

The net value of assets is reported on the FAFSA as of the day you file. Therefore, these strategies should be considered at any time, up until the day you file each FAFSA.

- **Save in the parents' name(s) rather than the student's.**

  Parent assets are assessed at only 5.6% and student assets at 20%. For example, saving $10,000 in a student's name adds $2,000 to the EFC. If it were in a parent's name, the EFC would only increase by $560, and only if the parent's asset protection allowance was exceeded.

- **Spend down student cash.**

  If money is already saved in a student's name, it can be kept out of the EFC formula by spending that money on things the student needs before filing the FAFSA. Examples include:

  - College necessities such as a computer, a car, sports equipment, art materials, dorm essentials, etc.
  - Services such as dental work or tutoring
  - Student enrichment such as internships or study abroad

- **Use student money before family money to pay any college costs.**

  If a student has significant assets, use them to pay tuition and other college costs before using parent cash or assets.

- **File your FAFSA right before a payday, when your cash reserves are lowest.**

- **Spend down parent assets that exceed the asset protection allowance *before* filing the FAFSA.**

  If you are secure enough financially, and/or were already planning a major purchase, it can be helpful to spend unprotected assets in any of the following ways:

  - Pay off consumer debt (credit cards, car loans, personal loans)
  - Purchase a new car or another big-ticket item you planned on buying anyway
  - Maximize your contributions to retirement accounts using unprotected assets rather than income

GOOD TO KNOW

The Savings Bond owner (not the beneficiary) must report the current value of the bond (not the face value) as an asset. You can get this information on the Treasury Department website by entering the type of bond and its issue date.

Parents making below $97,350 (single filers) or $153,550 (married filing jointly) can cash in bonds tax free or tax-reduced if they use the money to pay qualified education expenses. See IRS Publication 970 for more information.

GOOD TO KNOW

Retirement savings accounts aren't counted as assets on the FAFSA, but they are on the CSS profile.

Retirement funds may be withdrawn any time without penalty for qualified educational expenses (such as tuition and fees) for yourself, your spouse, your children, and your grandchildren; although, depending on the type of account, taxes may be due on the contributions and/or the earnings.

You should carefully crunch numbers if you plan on using retirement funds for college expenses because:

- The amount withdrawn may count as income the following year
- You are only allowed to take one educational federal income tax benefit per year

You can borrow from most retirement plans with the exception of IRAs, and you pay the interest on the loan to yourself. However, you must pay it back in five years or you'll have to pay the penalty for early withdrawal.

Maximize Your Free Money

Free money (grants and scholarships) is the financial aid you receive that does not have to be earned or paid back with interest. It is the only type of aid that actually reduces your Net Price.

State and Federal Grants are relatively small considering the high cost of a college education and are limited to students with high need. The majority of students will get little or no free government aid.

After awarding the maximum a student qualifies for in federal and state aid, most colleges try to meet at least *some* portion of the remaining Need with their own free money – either need-based grants or merit scholarships.

The amount of its own money a college awards depends on:

its financial aid policies
and
how much they want you to attend.

If you apply to colleges with generous financial aid policies *and* make it easy for them to see the contributions you would make to their community, you will greatly increase your chances of receiving a more generous college-funded award.

Apply to Colleges with Generous Financial Aid Policies

Colleges vary considerably in how generous they are, overall, with their financial aid. To get a pretty good idea of how generous a college is likely to be, follow these guidelines:

- **Apply to schools that are *generally* more generous.**

  Two statistics will help you identify these schools:

  - <u>The Average Percent of Need Met</u>

    About 3% of accredited 4-year colleges and universities pledge to meet 100% of student Need. Acceptance to these colleges is highly competitive and only possible for a small number of exceptional applicants. The remaining 97% of colleges meet a smaller, often much smaller, percentage of Need. For every college you are interested in, find out how much of a student's Need, on average, they meet.

  - <u>The Percentage of Students That Have 100% of Their Need Met</u>

    Although the vast majority of colleges do not meet 100% of the Need of *all* students, most will meet 100% of the Need of at least some of their students. Some schools value giving more money to fewer students rather than smaller amounts to a greater number in order to entice desirable students to enroll.

    If a school meets 100% of the need of only a few students, you are likely to get their average percentage of Need met. However, if it meets 100% of the Need of a larger number of students (e.g., > 20%), consider whether the qualities you can bring to the college (see below) could make you one of those students.

    See Appendix A for information on finding these two stats.

- **Apply to colleges that offer scholarships you qualify for.**

  Many college scholarships are competitive, but many others are awarded to all applicants based on hard data such as GPA or standardized test scores. Check the college's website to see what competitive scholarships you might receive and scholarships you would definitely receive based on your grades and test scores.

- **Look for a large endowment.**

  Large endowments are a sign of a college's financial strength and an indicator that they are likely to be more generous when awarding college grants. The larger the Endowment Per Student (EPS), the more of their own free money they are likely to award.

  Endowment statistics can be found in the college's Common Data Set, on U.S.News Best College's Website, or available from the college itself. See Appendix A for more information.

- **File your forms early.**

  It is common for colleges to award their best aid packages early, so file as soon as you can—certainly before the both the college's and your state's deadlines.

Apply to Colleges That Want You to Attend

The size of your college grants and scholarships will reflect both the college's financial aid policies and how much they want you to attend. When choosing colleges to apply to, think about what you bring to the college and how you can make it easy for admissions counselors to recognize your strengths. Following are some guidelines:

- **Apply to schools where your academic profile is significantly higher than those of students who typically apply.**

  Colleges always look to increase the academic strength of their student body and will sweeten the pot for academically strong applicants. You will almost certainly get more free money at schools where your GPA and standardized test scores are well above the average at that school.

- **Apply to Safety Schools that offer Honors Programs.**

  Often Honors Colleges, even at average schools, have programs as good as those found at elite schools. Admission into Honors Colleges often comes with large scholarships and/or grants.

GOOD TO KNOW

A Safety School is one where your academic qualifications are significantly better than those of previously accepted students. You are almost assured admission to these schools and will most likely receive a financial aid package far better than the average at that school.

Safety Schools may be in your best financial interest, but make sure they can also serve you academically and socially before applying.

- **Apply to schools where you offer diversity.**

  Colleges seek to increase the socioeconomic, gender, racial, ethnic, and geographic diversity of their campuses because it greatly enriches the campus community, both socially and academically. If your credentials are good and you can offer the kind of diversity the college is looking for, you will likely get a much better financial aid package.

  Worthy of note is the underappreciated value of geographic diversity. The majority of students on most campuses come from the region local to the college. If you come from an area not well-represented at a college, you may be awarded more generous aid. This holds for the school setting as well – rural students may be more attractive to an urban school, and vice versa.

- **Apply to schools that want the specific talent you can offer.**

  For example, a school that needs a hockey goalie or one that needs an oboe player for its orchestra might offer an excellent financial aid package to students who can fill those needs.

  For example, a school with an excellent music program might give an exceptional musician a much larger grant or scholarship than a music conservatory would (where all applicants would have exceptional musical ability).

- **Demonstrate your interest (and your maturity).**

  Colleges appreciate and notice students who actively seek greater and more individualized information about their school through personal outreach. Visiting a campus, scheduling an interview, and meeting with professors or coaches demonstrates initiative, maturity, and a sincere interest in attending a school. It makes an impression and can have an influence (sometimes significant) on both acceptance and financial aid. Be sure you arrange these visits through the admissions department, so admissions counselors remember you when your application arrives.

- **Look for programs the college wants to grow.**

  Most college applications ask about your intended major. If you are interested in majoring in a program the college has targeted for growth, and you indicate your interest in that major, you are more likely to get their attention, and an offer of more money. You rarely are required to major in the program you have noted on your application but check to be sure whether or not this is the case.

  This can also work for programs you don't intend to major in. For example, if the college is building a theater program, and you highlight your experience in theater and your intent to participate in college, you will be a more desirable applicant.

GOOD TO KNOW

- **Beware of applying Early Decision.**
  Acceptance rates are higher for Early Decision (ED) applicants, but if you have financial need, you may end up paying more. Colleges say that their ED financial aid packages are not different from their Regular Decision (RD) packages. However, since ED acceptances are binding, you'll never know how much free money they would have given you as an RD candidate. Much more importantly, you won't be able to compare financial aid packages from other schools, especially those that might have given you an outstanding financial aid package.
- **Beware of the waitlist.**
  Students who are waitlisted are more likely to receive less free money in their financial aid packages than those accepted earlier because the school has less money to award at that time, and less incentive to give you its best package.

CHAPTER 5

CALCULATING YOUR 4-YEAR PRICE TAG

- Decode Freshman Year Financial Aid Letters
- Your Annual Net Price Will Change
- The Cost of Borrowing
- Is It Truly a 4-Year Price Tag?

The 4-year price tag is often not considered when families compare colleges. If you are concerned about college costs, don't just look at the first year's costs. Instead, work to understand the cost for the entire time it will take to earn your degree. Tragically, many students borrow money to help pay for a year or two of college but drop out when they cannot afford to continue. The debt they acquire will haunt them for a decade or more, and with no college degree, they face reduced earnings with which to pay back this debt.

To get clear on your 4-year price tag and prepare for the full cost of your degree at a given college, you need to unscramble your freshman financial aid offers, learn how they might change over the following years, and include the cost of borrowing in your calculations.

Decode Freshman Year Financial Aid Letters

Financial aid letters from different colleges present information differently. Some are fairly straightforward, others terribly opaque, and, unfortunately, some can be deceptive. You will most likely have to decode these letters to fully understand your Net Price, the cost you actually pay to attend. This includes what you pay now and what you borrow and pay over time with interest.

The simplest way to calculate Net Price is:

COA – Free Money (grants, scholarships, discounts) = Net Price

However, financial aid letters are often unclear. A good financial aid letter should include:

- Your EFC, as calculated by the school based on the required financial aid forms
- The COA, broken down into tuition, fees, room and board, and a realistic estimate for indirect expenses like books, supplies, and personal expenses
- The types and amounts of aid awarded, written in plain language

Unfortunately, you will often have to fill in missing pieces, scrutinize numbers, and adjust calculations to arrive at your true Net Price. Appendix A includes a Financial Aid Comparison worksheet to help you clarify and compare your offers.

For example, consider the following sample financial aid letters for a student with an EFC of $12,000 and an outside scholarship of $1,000:

College A

Direct Charges	
Tuition and Fees	$12,500
Room and Board	$11,500
Indirect Costs	
Books and Supplies	$1,000
Personal Expenses	$600
Total Estimated COA	**$25,600**
Financial Aid	
University Grant	$1,000
State Grant	$400
Outside Scholarship	$1,000
Federal Direct Subsidized Loan	$3,500
Federal Direct Unsubsidized Loan	$2,000
Federal Work-Study	$1,200
Federal PLUS Loan Eligibility	$16,500
Total	**$25,600**

© 2021 College Admissions HQ

ANALYSIS

EFC is not listed.

COA grossly underestimates indirect costs. A good rule of thumb is to estimate $3,000 per year.

Free money

Financial Aid is misleading–They have included a Federal PLUS (parent) Loan. Parent loans are not financial aid.

This letter deceptively makes it look like your financial aid is equal to the COA.

College B

Estimated Cost of Attendance	**$60,900**
Tuition and Fees	$46,850
Room and Board	$10,550
Books and Supplies	$2,000
Personal Expenses	$1,500
Financial Aid	
Dean's Scholarship	$15,000
Outside Scholarship	$1,000
College Grant	$17,000
State Grant	$650
Federal Direct Subsidized Loan	$3,500
Federal Direct Unsubsidized Loan	$2,000
Federal Work-Study	$2,000
Total Financial Aid	**$41,150**
Estimated Remaining Balance	**$19,750**

© 2021 College Admissions HQ

ANALYSIS

EFC is not listed.

COA clearly listed, realistic, and broken down.

Financial Aid is clearly listed.

Free money

Remaining balance includes your EFC and a Gap but is not your Net Price, which will be higher because it also includes your federal loans and Work-Study.

To calculate your Net Price at College A:

Adjust the COA to $27,000 to reflect more realistic Indirect Costs. Subtract the free money awarded (grants and outside scholarship) from the COA:

COA – Free Money = Net Price

$27,000 - $2,400 = $24,600

Your Net Price at College A is $24,600, which includes:

EFC ($12,000) + Direct Loans ($5,500) +
Work-Study ($1,200) + Gap ($5,900)

To calculate Net Price at College B:

The listed COA is realistic and can be plugged into the equation. Subtract the free money awarded (grants and scholarships) from the COA.

COA – Free Money = Net Price

$60,900 - $33,650 = $27,250

Your Net Price at College B is $27,250 which includes:

EFC ($12,000) + Direct Loans ($5,500) +
Work-Study ($2,000) + Gap ($7,750)

Appealing a Financial Aid Award

Financial Aid Officers are usually willing to listen to *reasonable* arguments for more money if you are polite and follow their procedures.

Legitimate arguments include:

- A mistake in calculation or your EFC is not correct.
- A substantial difference in grant aid from a *similar* school---two colleges of the same *type* with similar *ranking*. Show them the competing offer, explain specifically why you would rather attend their school, and ask if they can help you better afford their school by increasing their financial support.
- A change in your financial situation. (A parent has lost a job, the family is paying unexpected medical costs, there was a death, an accident, a divorce etc.)
- A business or job with unpredictable income year to year. (Sometimes they will use an average income rather than the single year reported on the FAFSA.)
- Your family has a large student loan debt from an older sibling, or even a parent, that impacts your parents' ability to take on new debt for you.

SEE CHAPTER EIGHT

Colleges will not be allowed to have a policy to deny all financial aid appeals when the FAFSA changes.

Your Annual Net Price Will Change

Clarifying your freshman Net Price and multiplying by four isn't necessarily an accurate picture of the 4-year price tag. You will get a new financial aid package each year and even if your financial situation has not changed, your 2nd, 3rd, and 4th year financial aid packages can, and often do, look considerably different than your first-year year award.

How Net Price Changes

Increase in COA

Most colleges raise their COA 2-4% annually. This statistic is available for any college by checking the U.S. Department of Education's College Navigator website. Under the college's "Tuition, Fees, and Estimated Student Expenses" tab, you'll find the COA for the past four years and the percent increase for the past two years.

Use this information to estimate your COA for the next 3 years. Ask the college if they would protect current students from a future significant jump in COA.

Grants

Grants are based on financial Need and can come from the federal government, the state government, and the colleges themselves.

- **Federal Grants:** If you qualify for federal grants, they will remain similar all four years if your financial Need remains similar.
- **State Grants:** State grants change each year depending on the state's higher education budget and on how many students apply for aid, making it hard to predict future awards. Be conservative in your estimates. (See Appendix A for links to state grant programs.)
- **College Grants:** Some colleges award a similar grant each year if your financial need remains similar, and usually if you maintain a minimum GPA set by the college.

  However, many colleges practice "front-loading" -- giving generous college grants the first year to entice you to enroll, and then cutting their grant aid, sometimes significantly, in subsequent years. This dreadful practice has caught many students by surprise at a time when it is difficult to transfer to a different school. They often just pay the higher 2nd, 3rd, and 4th years' costs, significantly increasing the 4-year price tag.

  Ask the college:

  1. if your financial Need remains similar each year, will your college grants also remain similar. If not, how will future grants be determined?
  2. if college grants will increase enough to cover the increase in COA.
  3. if college grants will be awarded beyond the fourth year if extra time is needed to graduate.

Scholarships

Scholarships are based on merit, or other student attributes, and either come from outside organizations or from the colleges themselves.

- Outside Scholarships

  Scholarships you bring with you to college must be reported to the college and will be applied to your Need in your financial aid package

5

(See Chapter 3). These scholarships are often non-renewable (good only for one year).

Ask the college if your outside non-renewable scholarship will be covered in subsequent years by college grants, or will you be responsible for paying that amount.

- College Scholarships

  Scholarships awarded by the college may or may not be renewable and may come with participation or grade requirements.

  Ask the college:

  1. If a non-renewable scholarship will be covered in subsequent years by college grants.
  2. What requirements you must meet to keep a renewable scholarship and, if you lose it, will grants be awarded to cover that amount.
  3. If renewable scholarships can continue beyond four years if you take more than four years to graduate.

Self-Help Aid

Self-help aid includes federal and state student loans and Federal Work-Study. If you have financial Need, your financial aid package will almost always include this type of aid.

- Work-Study

  Work-Study awards usually remain similar each year, averaging $2,000, as long as your Need remains similar.

- State Loans

  State loan amounts may change depending on the practices of the individual state.

- Federal Direct Loans

  Federal Direct loan limits change even if your need remains the same.

  - $5,500 for freshman
  - $6,500 for sophomores
  - $7,500 for juniors and seniors

  Ask the college if your college grant will be reduced as federal loan limits rise. If so, your Net Price will also rise.

The Cost of Borrowing

The sad truth is that most families are unable to pay for college without taking out at least a few loans. Whether they are the Federal Direct Student Loans in your financial aid package, or private or PLUS loans needed to pay the EFC and/or Gap in financial aid, the cost of these loans adds considerably to the total price you pay for college. Your 4-year price tag to attend any college isn't complete without factoring in loan costs.

For example, if you need to borrow $35,000 over four years at 6% interest, a 10-year payback term makes the total cost of the loan $46,700—adding an additional $11,700 to the cost of your degree.

To get an estimate of how much borrowing will add to your overall Net Price use a student loan payment calculator (see Appendix A for links). Simply enter how much you will likely need to borrow each year and it will do the interest calculations for you.

Chapter 6 offers suggestions on how to reduce borrowing and keep the cost of unavoidable debt as low as possible.

Is It Truly a 4-Year Price Tag?

Don't take a 4-year graduation for granted at any college you might attend. Look up the 4-year graduation rate for the college at the US Department of Education's College Navigator website or at The Education Trust's College Results webpage. (Links available in Appendix A.) Be concerned about a college with an overall graduation rate below 60% and find out why this is the case.

Sometimes it's because the college offers many 5-year programs; or perhaps there is a large percentage of part-time students. There are many reasons why students don't graduate on time that will have no impact on you. But sometimes it's because the college itself does a poor job with advising or class scheduling, making it difficult for even an industrious student to finish in four years.

Adding unplanned semesters to your education drastically increases your overall costs, both in expenses and the lost wages you would have earned had you graduated on time.

CHAPTER 6

ADDITIONAL WAYS TO SHAVE COLLEGE COSTS

- Graduate Early (or, at Least, on Time)
- Ways to Reduce Costs
- Wisely Manage Your Debt
- Wisely Use Your Tax Benefits

A penny saved is not only a penny earned, but a penny not borrowed with capitalized, compounded interest. Following are some ideas that will net from moderate to truly significant savings in overall college costs.

Graduate Early (or, at Least, on Time)

One of the most obvious, common-sense ways to save the most money is to graduate a semester or two early. You'll save thousands, probably tens of thousands of dollars and can still participate in the college's graduation ceremony. Many of the suggestions in this chapter offer alternative and less expensive ways to earn the credits you need to graduate early.

If graduating early isn't possible, it's crucial to graduate *on time*. Adding a semester or more to the time it takes to earn your degree greatly increases your overall Net Price. Add to that the lost time in post-graduate wages, and the financial picture looks even worse.

GOOD TO KNOW

Graduating on time isn't as easy as it may sound. According to the National Center for Education Statistics, the average 4-year graduation rate at public colleges is only 36% and at private colleges, only 54%. Stay on track by actively engaging with advising programs, fully understanding graduation requirements, and planning each semester's class schedule well ahead, even years ahead, to be sure you can take all the classes needed to get your degree.

Ways to Reduce the Costs

Tuition

Tuition is the biggest item on your college bill. It's only reasonable that earning some of the credits required for graduation in alternative, less expensive ways will save you loads of money. Some of the following strategies can be implemented while in high school, some while in college, and some can be used at either time.

1. **Maximize Your Course Load**

   Sometimes colleges charge tuition per credit hour, but usually full-time students are charged per semester for a range of credits they can earn. If you are paying tuition per semester rather than per credit, it only makes sense to take the maximum number of credits you can *successfully* manage each semester. You definitely don't want to overload, get poor grades, or burn out. But for semesters when it's possible, this strategy can help you shave off some of the time it takes to earn your degree.

2. **Test Out**

   Most colleges allow students to earn college credits through testing. Check with each college to fully understand their policies before planning to use this strategy.

   The two testing programs for college credit, CLEP (College Level Examination Program) and AP (Advanced Placement), are both administered by the College Board.

   College Level Examination Program (CLEP)

   CLEP tests assess your proficiency at the college-level in 36 subject areas. Nearly 3000 colleges and universities accept CLEP scores for college credit, but each school has its own policies regarding which exams they accept, what scores earn credit, and the total number of CLEP credits they will grant. You study for and take CLEP tests on your own time while in high school or college. Each test costs $89 and you can earn between 3 – 6 credits per test.

   Advanced Placement (AP)

   AP courses offer high school students college-level material in 38 subject areas. Classes are taught either in your high school or online. Nearly all colleges in the U.S. accept AP scores for credit and/or placement into higher level classes. However, each college has its own policies regarding which exams and scores they will accept. AP exams are administered each May and cost $96 each.

3. **Dual Enrollment (DE)**

   Dual Enrollment (DE) programs allow 11th and 12th-grade high school students to enroll in one or two college classes per semester at a nearby college. Tuition is often significantly discounted, and sometimes even free, depending on the arrangement the college has with your high school or state.

Not all colleges will accept all DE credits. Some object to credits that count towards your high school diploma, or credits earned in classes that were taught in your high school by high school teachers, rather than on college campuses. As with CLEP and AP, check with each college you are interested in attending to learn their policies on DE credit transfer.

GOOD TO KNOW

Earning college credits while in high school not only allows you to enter college with a semester or more under your belt, it also adds shine to your college applications, boosting your chances of acceptance and more free money in your financial aid package.

4. **Online Courses**

The blossoming number of online courses available from accredited colleges, universities, and community colleges makes this option for earning college credits tempting. Sometimes you can enroll while in your junior or senior year of high school and bring credits with you to college. But another option is to fit in a few general education courses during summer or winter breaks while attending college.

As with any of these strategies, it only works if the college you attend will accept these credits. It is also important to compare the cost of taking the course(s) online versus what it would cost to take it at your college.

GOOD TO KNOW

This strategy is especially helpful if you are short a class or two for graduation. Rather than going to college for an additional semester, see if you can take those classes online or at another local, cheaper college during a break.

5. **Community College**

If you are fortunate enough to live within commuting distance of a community college, consider earning credits there for a year or so before transferring to a 4-year college.

Tuition is significantly lower at community colleges than at most 4-year colleges. As a commuter, you'll also save a bundle on room and board costs, which range from $6,000 - $18,000 per year.

There are several ways to use this strategy:

- Earn credits either while in high school or after graduation and transfer them in to a 4-year college.
- Earn your 2-year associate degree at the community college and immediately transfer to a 4-year college for your bachelor's degree.
- Earn your 2-year associate degree and enter the job market. If you still want to earn your bachelor's degree, and there are plenty of good reasons for that, consider doing that while you are employed and earning money. Your employer may foot some or all of the bill for your college education.

If you plan to transfer community college credits to a 4-year college, make sure all those credits will be accepted for your general education requirements and/or those required for your intended major. Established transfer programs between community colleges and 4-year colleges are especially helpful, but also understand what minimum grades are required.

6. **Study Abroad**

The United States is one of the most expensive countries in the world in which to attend college. Higher education is much cheaper, or even free for non-citizens at many excellent universities worldwide. Whether you would like to earn your degree abroad, or simply study abroad for a semester or two, this option requires thoughtful planning.

Some tips for using this strategy include:

- Don't enroll through a study abroad company. It is much cheaper to enroll directly with the university or study abroad through your home college.
- Be sure classes are taught in English or in a language you understand and/or want to learn.
- You can still receive U.S. federal financial aid at some universities outside the U.S. More information is available on the federal Student Aid website.
- Include travel expenses when comparing costs.
- On-campus housing, when available, is often much cheaper overseas, but if you plan to live off campus, include the cost of living when comparing costs. The website Expatistan offers a simple calculator.

- Often degree programs outside the U.S. are shorter, saving even more money.
- Professions that require U.S. licensure such as medicine and law may not recognize degrees earned outside the U.S.
- Carefully research any university of interest, but particularly those outside the U.S. Check a university's worldwide ranking at Times Higher Education and QS World Rankings.

See Appendix A for links.

Fees

There is no way to avoid paying fees whether you use the services or not. Fees can add up to as much as $1,000 per semester and include those for orientation, labs, technology, health and wellness, athletics, activities, and graduation. Examine Cost of Attendance pages on a college's website to fully understand the fees they charge.

Room (Housing) and Board (Food)

Housing away from home is the second largest college expense. The average annual cost for room and board at public colleges is $11,700, and $13,200 at private colleges.

Housing: If you are able to live at home and commute to college, you will save thousands each year. If you cannot commute from home, consider sharing off-campus housing with other students. Often this saves about half the costs of on-campus room and board.

There are good reasons to live on campus and if that is important to you, here are two ways you might be able to reduce that cost:

- Choose the cheapest type of housing the school offers—for example "triples" could be cheaper than "doubles;" and traditional rooms could be cheaper than suites or college apartments.
- Become a Resident Assistant (RA). Sometimes called Resident Advisors, Community Advisors, or Community Assistants, RAs are given significant compensation—the most lucrative housing savings you can get – in exchange for providing support to a specific group of students in a dorm. Most colleges give RAs a free single room (worth $7,000 a year or more), but many offer additional perks such as free meals (worth approximately $4,500), and/or a stipend (up to a few thousand dollars).

Board: Going hungry should never be the way college students save money, but, sadly, many do. Students can, and should, eat a healthy diet while in school, and still find ways to be frugal.

- **Living On Campus**

  The average cost of a cafeteria meal is $7.50, more than twice the cost of preparing meals yourself. In addition, many students mindlessly pay for meals they aren't using in a deluxe meal plan. If you are living on campus and want to save money on food, choose the most flexible meal plan at the lowest price. And when you do eat in the cafeteria, eat up! If permitted, take some portable fruit like bananas and apples with you when you go. It's pretty easy to eat a simple but healthy meal or two made in your dorm room each day, especially when you have a refrigerator, freezer, and/or microwave.

- **Living Off Campus**

  Plan meals ahead of time, buy good quality food, pack meals if you will be eating on campus, and limit the amount of food you purchase on campus.

No matter where you are living, limit the number of meals you eat out.

Books, Supplies, and Personal Expenses

The COA includes an average for the cost of books, supplies, and personal expenses, but this is a real wild card. Education-related expenses such as books and supplies vary widely depending on your major. Travel expenses are dependent on the distance and how often you want to go home. However, every student can save some money using some of the following tips:

Textbooks: Textbooks can cost hundreds of dollars each semester.

- You may be able to share the cost and use of a book with another student(s) in the class.
- See if a required book is available to borrow from your school library or is available as open-source material.
- Renting textbooks from your college bookstore or online is usually a fraction of the cost of purchasing them.
- Purchase textbooks online rather than from your college bookstore.
- Sell the books you no longer need to the best paying buyer – either another student, your college bookstore, or an online retailer.

SEE CHAPTER EIGHT

When the FAFSA changes, the COA will include an allowance for books and supplies that reflects the costs associated with the student's major.

GOOD TO KNOW

Some of the many reliable websites for textbook rentals and purchase include Chegg, Amazon Textbooks, ValoreBooks, and CampusBooks. Shipping both ways is usually free. Studentrate.com compares the rates of various online retailers. See Appendix A for links.

Travel

It's hard to decide whether or not to bring a car to campus. The advantages to bringing a car are independence, peace of mind that you won't be riding with other drivers, and easy travel to and from home. The disadvantage, however, is that it's costly:

- Insurance companies often discount premiums if the car stays home.
- Parking can be very expensive and difficult to find.
- You may be chauffeuring friends around – sometimes even for big "asks" like rides to the airport or train station.

Without a car, you have to pay attention to the cost of transportation home. You can save money by purchasing plane, train, or bus tickets in advance; using student discounts; or finding students who have cars and live near your home and offer to share the expense of a ride home.

GOOD TO KNOW

Look for student discounts on entertainment, transportation, groceries, restaurants, clothing, technology, and other goods and services both locally and online. Studentrate.com is a great place to find deals.

"Free" Stuff

Take advantage of the no-cost activities, movies, entertainment, services, and technology (sometimes including laptops) available to you on-campus. These things really aren't "free" because you have paid for them with your fees, but they feel free, and at least they don't cost you any more money.

Take the Work-Study Job

Work-Study is a federal program of on-campus employment for students who have financial Need. There are significant advantages to Work-Study employment:

- The money you make helps you take on less debt
- A variety of jobs are available
- Hours are usually adjustable, especially in times of stress
- It pays at least minimum wage and you can earn, on average, $2,000 per year
- It's a great way to fund your books, supplies, and personal expenses throughout the year
- Earnings do not affect your EFC

GOOD TO KNOW

Employment while in college can affect your ability to graduate early or even on-time. If your job makes it impossible for you to take the course load necessary to graduate on time, weigh the amount of money you will earn against the extra expenses of additional time in school.

Stick to a Budget

Calculate your expected costs, allow for bumps along the way, and set up a spending firewall. One great way to stay on budget is to use cash rather than credit or debit cards for expenses.

Wisely Manage Your Debt

Use Tuition Payment Plans to Reduce Borrowing

Not all colleges offer them, but when available, tuition payment plans allow you to pay all or a portion of each year's tuition in 10 – 12 monthly interest-free installments. Any amount of tuition paid this way saves the fees and interest you would otherwise have to pay on loans.

Parents may believe they don't have extra money available each month to put towards a tuition payment plan. However, while the student is living at college, you can save hundreds of dollars on food, utilities, car insurance, and other costs each month–money that can go into a tuition payment plan.

And the reality is, payback on parent loans usually starts as soon as the funds are disbursed, so you will have to find the money to make those payments anyway.

Keep an Eye on Your Loans

The only student loan that doesn't accrue interest while you are in school is the Federal Direct *Subsidized* Loan. All other loans will start charging interest the day they are disbursed. You can allow interest to capitalize (that is, added to your principal and the total amount you owe) or you can pay it as you go. Paying just the interest on your loans (or more, if possible) will save you thousands of dollars over the life of the loan.

Other money-saving pay-back tips include:

- Make bi-weekly rather than monthly payments after graduation. This will add one additional payment each year, which can save a bundle in overall loan interest.
- Apply extra payments toward the principal with the highest interest rates first. If all your loans have the same interest rate, apply extra payments to the loan with the highest total principal balance.
- Use Auto-Pay for Repayment to Reduce Interest Rates. Most lenders will offer at least 0.25% reduction in interest if you auto-pay your loans, saving $525 over ten years on a $35,000 loan.

GOOD TO KNOW

You will pay origination fees on all Federal Direct and PLUS loans, and many private student loans. This is the cost a borrower must pay when first taking out the loan. Origination fees on federal loans range from 1% - 4.5% and are usually deducted from the loan amount before it is disbursed.

For example, the average annual PLUS loan is $16,450. The fee of approximately 4.3%, $700, goes to the federal government and $15,750 goes to the school. Over four years that amounts to $2,800 in origination fees alone.

Wisely Use Your Tax Benefits

- The federal government offers two education tax credits for those who qualify:
    - The American Opportunity Tax Credit (AOTC) allows a maximum $2,500 credit per year for four years.
    - The Lifetime Learning Credit (LLC) is worth up to $2,000 per year, per student, and is available for an unlimited number of years.

  Both credits phase out at a modified AGI of $80,000-$90,000 (single) and $160,000 - $180,000 (married, filing jointly).

  A family can take either the AOTC or the LLC for the same child in the same tax year, but not both.

- The federal government also allows taxpayers to deduct up to $2,500 in student loan interest from their taxable income.

  The deduction is phased out at a modified AGI between $70,000 and $85,000 ($140,000 and $170,000 if you file a joint return).

Either set aside any tax benefits for the following year's tuition or apply them to existing loans.

More information on federal education tax benefits can be found in IRS Publication 970.

CHAPTER 7

THE FAMILY CONVERSATION ABOUT MONEY

The first six chapters of this book give you the information and tools you need to realistically predict what any college of interest will cost you. But is everyone in your family on the same page about how to meet those costs? Is everyone clear about:

- WHO is responsible for what costs
- HOW those costs will be paid
- WHEN that responsibility will start (and stop)

Don't wait for your financial aid letters to arrive to figure this out! Before even *applying* to any college, clarify both parent and student expectations and make a plan that is consistent with your family's needs, resources, goals, and values.

Families often have a hard time talking about money, and conversations about college costs between anxious parents and starry-eyed college-bound high school students can be especially difficult. However, when tackling a financial challenge as large as paying for college, the benefits of establishing a clear understanding are well worth the effort.

The following questions can help launch your discussion:

- Who will pay for admissions tests?

  ACT, SAT, and AP testing is costly. How many admissions tests can you afford? Do you qualify for testing fee waivers and how do you get them? Appendix A includes a worksheet to help you keep track of and budget for these costs.

- Who will pay application costs?

  Application costs can be significant and add up fast. How many applications can you afford? Do you qualify for application fee waivers and how do you get them? Appendix A includes a worksheet to help you keep track of and budget for these costs.

- Are parents willing and/or able to help pay for college?
  - What dollar amount of parent income and/or assets can be applied to college costs?
  - Are parents willing to borrow money to help pay for college?

    If yes:
    - Will the student be expected to help pay those loans back?
    - Would parents borrow PLUS or private loans?

        - How much total parent debt is reasonable?
            - What would the actual monthly payment be on that amount?
            - What is the expected payback period for these loans?
    - Are parents willing to co-sign private student education loans issued in the student's name?
        - Who will pay those back?
        - Will the student be expected to remove the parent co-signer from the loan if possible? (A co-signer often can be removed once the student is making sufficient income and after making a set number of on-time payments.)
- Are students willing and/or expected to help pay for college?
    - What dollar amount of student income and/or assets can be applied to college costs?
    - Will students borrow the maximum in Federal Direct and state student loans?
        - What would the total monthly payment be on those loans?
        - Will parents help the student pay back those loans?
    - Will students borrow private loans (with a parent co-signer)?
        - Who is responsible to pay those back?
        - What would the total monthly payment be on those loans?
    - How much total student debt (government and private loans) is reasonable?
        - What would the actual monthly payment be on that amount?
        - What is the expected payback period for these loans?

Parents should consider their retirement plans and the needs of their other children when determining what they can realistically contribute to the cost of one child's college.

Students should consider their lifestyle and career choices when determining how much debt they can reasonably take on.

CHANGES TO THE FAFSA AND FINANCIAL AID

To Be Fully Implemented by the 2024-25 School Year

- The FAFSA Simplification Act
- Changes to the FAFSA Experience
- Changes to Need Analysis
- Changes to Pell Grant Eligibility
- Changes that Increase Accessibility to Federal Student Aid
- Other Changes
- The Upshot

Many changes are coming to the FAFSA and to college financial aid after the 2022-23 school year. They are intended to make financial aid easier to access, increase funding to the neediest students, and allow more leeway for college financial aid officers to adjust financial aid packages.

This chapter presents a summary of what to expect, but at the time of this book's publication, a few details and implementation dates are still unclear. As new information becomes available, updates will be posted at https://collegeadmissionshq.org/PayLessForCollegeResources.

The FAFSA Simplification Act

The FAFSA Simplification Act is part of The Consolidated Appropriations Act 2021 (H.R. 133), a $2.3 trillion spending bill signed into law in December of 2020. It calls for key changes to Federal Student Aid, including the FAFSA (Free Application for Federal Student Aid) form, need analysis, Pell Grant eligibility, and many other financial aid policies and procedures. It will affect every school that participates in the Federal Title IV program (student financial aid) and every state that uses FAFSA data to award state aid.

Changes will be phased in over the next two years and will be fully implemented by the 2024-25 school year. Federal, state, and college financial aid officials are in the process of translating the legislative changes into practice.

GOOD TO KNOW

2021-22 high school seniors should expect the FAFSA to be a little different each year until their third year in college.

Changes to the FAFSA Experience

There Will Be Fewer Questions

The current FAFSA has 108 questions. The new FAFSA will have only 36 questions, although some will have multiple parts.

> *The lowest income families will have the fewest questions to answer, making the FAFSA significantly easier to complete for this group of students. However, because skip-logic in the electronic FAFSA form skips over questions not relevant to the student, the majority of*

> *students never answered many of the original 108 questions anyway, so their experience with the new FAFSA will be similar.*

"Expected Family Contribution" (EFC) Will Be Replaced with "Student Aid Index" (SAI)

The Student Aid Index (SAI) is largely just a new name for Expected Family Contribution (EFC). The change in terminology is intended to avoid the false impression that the EFC is *all* you are expected to contribute to the Cost of Attendance (COA). Instead, the SAI will indicate the student's eligibility for financial aid. Like the EFC, the SAI will be determined by an assessment of your income and assets based on information you provide on your FAFSA. Colleges will still calculate your Need with the same equation:

Need = COA - SAI (formerly EFC)

> *Regardless of what it is called, the SAI, just like the EFC, will represent the minimum amount of money you (and your family) will be expected to pay for college in a given year. Most families pay more than their EFC, and most will pay more than their SAI.*

Income Information Will Be Directly Imported from the IRS

The current IRS Data Retrieval Tool is cumbersome and not everybody qualifies to use it. The new FAFSA will allow you to authorize direct transfer of relevant information from the IRS without leaving the FAFSA form and removes restrictions on who can use it.

Changes to Need Analysis

The Cost of Attendance (COA) Will Be Expanded

The published sticker price to attend any college or university is called its Cost of Attendance (COA). The COA must be published on the college's website and has been expanded as illustrated in the chart below.

> *Because your financial Need will be determined by the equation, COA - SAI = Need, a larger COA will make you eligible for more financial aid than under the current COA guidelines.*

Costs Included in the College's Cost of Attendance (COA)		Current COA	New COA
Direct Expenses	Tuition	✓	✓
	Fees	✓	✓
	On-Campus Room and Board	✓	✓
Indirect Expenses	*Books and Course Materials	✓	✓
	Personal Expenses	✓	✓
	Off-Campus Housing Allowance, Including Students Living at Home or Studying Abroad		✓
	Allowance for 3 Meals a Day Including Students Living Off-Campus or at Home		✓
	Allowance for Transportation, Including Commuting Students		✓
	Allowance for Students in Co-Op Programs		✓
	Allowance for Dependent Care for Students with Dependents		✓
	Federal Student Loan Fees		✓
	Fees for Obtaining Professional Licensure, Certification, or Credentials		✓
	Allowances for Costs Associated with Disabilities		✓
	*The current COA includes an average for the cost of books and supplies. The new COA will include an allowance for books and supplies that is specific for the course of study.		

© 2021 College Admissions HQ

8

The SAI Can Be *Less* than Zero

- The lowest SAI will be -$1,500. (The lowest EFC was zero.)
- Independent students who are non-tax filers and dependent students whose parents are non-tax filers will have an automatic -$1,500 SAI.
- Any student who qualifies for the Maximum Pell Grant (see below) will receive an automatic zero SAI (unless the student has a negative SAI, in which case the negative number will be the SAI).

A student who does not qualify for an *automatic* zero or -$1,500 SAI can have a *calculated* zero or negative SAI.

Your financial Need will be determined by the equation COA – SAI = Need. A negative SAI means you will be eligible for financial aid greater than the college's COA. A zero SAI means you will be eligible for financial aid equal to the college's COA.

> *If you are eligible for financial aid greater than the COA you will not get larger federal grants or loans, but federal aid will not be reduced if you receive other types of financial aid.*

Parent Contribution to the SAI Will Not Be Divided by the Number of Children in College

Parents pay only one contribution to the EFC, and the EFC formula divides it by the number of children attending college at the same time. By contrast, parents will be responsible to pay their full SAI contribution for each child in college.

> *This major change will hurt families with more than one child in college. Under the new formula, the SAI will be roughly double for families with two children in college, triple for those with three, etc.*

The Definition of "Independent Student" Will Be Modified

Currently, a student is considered independent if he or she is at least 24 years old; married (or separated, but not divorced); enrolled in a graduate or professional program; providing more than half the financial support for a dependent child(ren) or other dependents; an orphan, in foster care, or a ward of the court; in legal guardianship or an emancipated minor; homeless (or at risk of being homeless); currently serving in the Armed Forces or a veteran of the Armed Forces.

The new FAFSA will modify the definition of "married" to be "married and *not* separated," and will add "unable to contact the parent(s) or it could be unsafe to do so" to the list of criteria.

Some Untaxed Income Will No Longer Be Reported

Many types of untaxed income that currently help determine the EFC will not be included in the SAI Need analysis as outlined below.

> *The elimination of these types of untaxed income in Need analysis will increase aid eligibility for many students. However, some colleges may still require that parents and students continue to report all untaxed income on the CSS Profile or on the college's own forms.*

<table>
<tr><th>Types of Untaxed Income</th><th>Parents of Dependent Students</th><th>Dependent and Independent Students</th></tr>
<tr><td>Child Support
Worker's Compensation
Disability and Veterans Benefits
Military and Clergy Allowances
Untaxed Portions of HSAs</td><td colspan="2">Will not be reported as income on the FAFSA</td></tr>
<tr><td rowspan="2">Cash Support, Gifts, or Any Money Paid on the Student's Behalf by Anyone Other Than a Parent Whose Income Is Reported</td><td rowspan="2">N/A</td><td>Will not be reported as income on the FAFSA</td></tr>
<tr><td>This change will allow grandparents, or anyone else, to help pay college costs, including distributions from 529 accounts, without those contributions being assessed as student untaxed income.</td></tr>
</table>

© 2021 College Admissions HQ

Three Allowances Against Income Will Change

Allowances against income reduce your reported income, decrease your SAI, and increase your financial aid. The coming changes will benefit some families and hurt others as illustrated in the chart below.

<table>
<tr><th>Allowances Against Income</th><th>Parents of Dependent Students</th><th>Dependent and Independent Students</th></tr>
<tr><td rowspan="2">State Tax Allowance</td><td colspan="2">Eliminated</td></tr>
<tr><td colspan="2">This change will make the SAI a little larger, which will decrease aid eligibility. It will especially hurt families that live in high tax states such as NY, NJ, CT, CA, MA, MN, OR, MD, who, in the current formula, are given a state tax allowance of between 6-10% of total income.</td></tr>
<tr><td rowspan="2">Income Protection Allowance (IPA)</td><td>Will increase 20% over the 2021-22 IPA, and will no longer be reduced by having more than one child in college</td><td>Will increase 35% over the 2021-22 IPA (will increase 60% for single independent students with dependents)</td></tr>
<tr><td colspan="2">These increases will make the SAI a little smaller, increasing aid eligibility. Student income above IPA is assessed at 50%, so increases in IPA will remove disincentives for student employment.</td></tr>
<tr><td rowspan="2">Employee Expense Allowance</td><td colspan="2">Will be adjusted annually for inflation</td></tr>
<tr><td colspan="2">This change will make the SAI a little smaller, which will increase aid eligibility.</td></tr>
</table>

© 2021 College Admissions HQ

Some Filers Will Be Exempt from Reporting Assets

Independent students and parents of a dependent student (and that student) will be exempt from reporting assets if:

- The student qualifies for the Maximum Pell Grant
- They have an adjusted gross income of less than $60,000 ($50,000 in the EFC formula) (and do not file a tax return with lettered schedules A – H or file a Schedule C with net business income loss or gain over $10,000).

The effect of assets on the size of the SAI will remain relatively low as compared to the effect of income, as was the case with the EFC formula. However, the $10,000 increase in income limits means more families will be exempt from reporting assets and will have a simpler FAFSA to complete.

Child Support Will be Reported as a Parent Asset

The EFC formula requires that Child Support be reported as parent income and is assessed up to 47%. As a parent asset in the SAI formula, child support will be assessed at a maximum of 5.6%.

GOOD TO KNOW

Even though available assets will be *reported* differently, there will be no change to the way they will be *assessed*:

- Parents at a maximum of 5.64%, with a small asset protection allowance
- Dependent students and independent students with no dependents, at a flat 20% with no asset protection allowance
- Independent students with dependents at a maximum of 3.29%

There also will be no change to how parent Asset Protection Allowance tables are calculated, which means these allowances are likely to continue to decline.

The Definition of Family Size Will Change

Family size will be a factor in calculating both the Income Protection Allowance and the Maximum and Minimum Pell Grant eligibility. Family size will be defined as described below.

- Dependent Students
    - If parents are married, family size will include the student, both parents, and any dependents (as defined by the IRS) of the parents for the tax year being reported
    - If the parents are separated or divorced, family size will include the student, the parent who will report income, and any of that parent's dependents (as defined by the IRS) for the tax year being reported
    - If the parents are divorced and the reporting parent is remarried, family size will include the student, that parent, that parent's dependents (as defined by the IRS), the new spouse, and any dependent of the new spouse (as defined by the IRS) if the new spouse's income is included in determining parent available income for the tax year being reported
- Independent Students
    - If the student is married, family size will include the student, the spouse, and any dependents of the student (as defined by the IRS) for the tax year being reported
    - If the student is divorced or separated, family size will include only the student and any dependent of the student (as defined by the IRS) for the tax year being reported

GOOD TO KNOW

The new FAFSA will ask for confirmation that the family size indicated on the parents' (or independent student's) prior-prior year's tax return is accurate. If it has changed, it must be amended to reflect the applicant's current family size.

The Divorced or Separated Parent Who is Required to Report Will Change

The current rules require reporting by the custodial parent (the one the student lived with most of the time). The new FAFSA will require the parent who provides the most financial support in the prior-prior year to report income and assets on the FAFSA regardless of where the student resides. If parents provide equal support, the parent with the higher income will have to report.

> *This change closes a loophole that may have been used by some families to enable the parent with lower income to report.*

Changes to Pell Grant Eligibility

For 2022-23, Pell Grant eligibility still depends on your EFC, which is determined largely by your income and to a lesser extent, your assets. Appendix A includes the 2021-22 Pell Grant awards table. In January 2022, the 2022-23 Pell Grant awards table will be posted at https://collegeadmissionshq.org/PayLessForCollegeResources.

With the coming changes, Maximum and Minimum Pell Grant awards will have different eligibility criteria from other federal financial aid.

- <u>Maximum Pell Grants will automatically be awarded to:</u>
    - Dependent students whose parents are non-tax filers
    - Independent students who are non-tax filers
    - Dependent or independent students under the age of 33 whose parent or guardian died in the line of duty serving as a member of the Armed Forces post-9/11 or died in the line of duty while performing as a public safety officer
- <u>Other students will qualify for the Maximum or Minimum Pell Grants based on:</u>
    - Family size
    - Family type (single parent, two-parent, non-parent student)
    - Prior-prior year adjusted gross income (AGI) as a percentage of the prior-prior year's Federal Poverty Level (FPL)

The tables below show the income levels that will qualify for Maximum and Minimum Pell Grants if changes are fully implemented for the 2023-24 FAFSA. They are based on 2021 the FPL, the tax year reported on the 2023-24 FAFSA.

DEPENDENT STUDENTS

		Maximum Pell		Minimum Pell	
^Family Size	2021 Federal Poverty Level	Single-Parent Household *AGI < 225% FPL	Two-Parent Household AGI < 175% FPL	Single-Parent Household AGI < 325% FPL	Two-Parent Household AGI < 275% FPL
1	$12,880	---	---	---	---
2	$17,420	$39,195	---	$56,615	---
3	$21,960	$49,410	$38,430	$71,370	$60,390
4	$26,500	$59,625	$46,375	$86,125	$72,875
5	$31,040	$69,840	$54,320	$100,880	$85,360
6	$35,580	$80,055	$62,265	$115,635	$97,845
7	$40,120	$90,270	$70,210	$130,390	$110,330
8	$44,660	$100,485	$78,155	$145,145	$122,815

^Families/households with more than 8 persons, add $4,540 for each additional person.
*Parent(s) AGI from 2021; Income must be greater than $0

© 2021 College Admissions HQ

INDEPENDENT STUDENTS

		Maximum Pell			Minimum Pell		
^Family Size	2021 Federal Poverty Level	Single-Parent Household *AGI < 225% FPL	Two-Parent Household AGI < 175% FPL	Non-Parent Student AGI < 175% FPL	Single-Parent Household AGI < 400% FPL	Two-Parent Household AGI < 350% FPL	Non-Parent Student AGI < 275% FPL
1	$12,880	---	---	$22,540	---	---	$35,420
2	$17,420	$39,195	---	$30,485	$69,680	---	$47,905
3	$21,960	$49,410	$38,430	---	$87,840	$76,860	---
4	$26,500	$59,625	$46,375	---	$106,000	$92,750	---
5	$31,040	$69,840	$54,320	---	$124,160	$108,640	---
6	$35,580	$80,055	$62,265	---	$142,320	$124,530	---
7	$40,120	$90,270	$70,210	---	$160,480	$140,420	---
8	$44,660	$100,485	$78,155	---	$178,640	$156,310	---

^Families/households with more than 8 persons, add $4,540 for each additional person.
*Student household AGI from 2021; Income must be greater than $0

© 2021 College Admissions HQ

- Pell Grants between the Maximum and the Minimum will be determined by subtracting the student's SAI from the Maximum Pell

Negative SAIs will be treated as zero in this equation.

If a student's SAI is larger than the Maximum Pell or the difference is less than the Minimum Pell, that student will not qualify for any Pell Grant.

- Eligibility for Pell Grants will be restored to students who:
    - Were unable to complete their program of study due to their school closing
    - Were falsely certified as eligible to receive federal financial aid
    - Had their loans discharged in a successful borrower defense claim
    - Are incarcerated and enrolled in a qualifying program

Changes that Increase Accessibility to Federal Student Aid

- **Selective Service Registration Will No Longer Be Required for Male Students to Access Federal Financial Aid**
- **Drug Convictions Will No Longer Disqualify Students**

  It is too late to remove these two questions from the 2022-23 FAFSA form, but colleges have been instructed on how to process the forms in order to eliminate their effect.

- **Barriers for Homeless and Foster Care Youth Will Be Reduced**

  There will be a simplified process for these students to file the FAFSA without parental information and to request professional judgement regarding independent status.

- **The FAFSA Will Be Available in More Languages**

  The current FAFSA is available in English and Spanish only. The new FASFSA will be available in at least 11 languages.

- **It Will No Longer Be Legal to Charge a Fee to Help File the FAFSA**

Other Changes

- **Time Limitations on Eligibility for Federal Direct Subsidized Loans Have Been Repealed**

  Starting with loans disbursed after July 1, 2021, there will be no limit on the period of time a borrower can receive Federal Direct Subsidized Loans. Under the current rules, a student can qualify to receive Direct Subsidized Loans for a maximum of 150% of the published length of the program of study.

Repealing this limitation allows students to take more time to complete their degree and still access Direct Subsidized Loans. However, the lifetime maximum Direct Loan limits will not change (see Chapter 2).

- **Colleges Will Be Prohibited from Maintaining a Policy That Denies All Financial Aid Appeals**
- **The Authority of Financial Aid Administrators Will Be Expanded**

  With the proper documentation of hardship, college financial aid officers will have the authority to adjust a student's financial aid eligibility by adjusting the COA, the values used to calculate the student's SAI and Pell Grant eligibility, and the student's dependency status. This authority will cover a broader range of special circumstances including natural disasters and emergencies; recession or economic downturn; substantial losses in business, investments, or real estate; recent unemployment; excessive medical or dependent care costs; severe disability of a student or parent, etc.

- **Approximately $1.6 Billion in Outstanding Loans to 45 HBCUs (Historically Black Colleges and Universities) Has Been Forgiven**

  Removing this burden will help these schools rebuild aging infrastructure, improve their retention rates and academic outcomes for their students, and provide more funding for their own college-awarded scholarships and grants.

8

The Upshot

The FAFSA Simplification ACT was intended to encourage more students to file the FAFSA and to increase aid to the neediest students. It will likely succeed in making the FAFSA simpler for most students to file, but navigating financial aid is about to get more complicated.

Students with high need will qualify for more need-based aid, and the neediest will get a healthier portion of their college costs covered at public colleges and universities.

But for most students, federal grants and loans still will not cover the COA at most colleges, and the size of college grants still depends on each college's financial aid policies. The vast majority of colleges do not even come close to meeting a student's full Need.

Middle- and upper-income students aren't likely to see much, if any, reduction in what they are expected to pay for college, and because of certain changes to the need analysis formula, some families will be expected to pay *much* more.

The FAFSA Simplification Act was not intended to, nor does it, address the staggering cost of college and the associated student and parent debt crisis. Sadly, most families will still be expected to pay more than their SAI (some much more) and will continue to take on significant debt in order to do so.

With or without the FAFSA Simplification Act, the best defense against soaring college costs and drowning in college debt is to take advantage of the tools provided in this book:

- Get a realistic expectation of what any college of interest would cost you, before you even apply
- Take advantage of any cost-saving strategies that can work for you
- Plan ahead for the college costs you will likely be responsible for

LINKS, RESOURCES, AND WORKSHEETS

- Links
- Resources
    - Guide to the Common Data Set
    - Pell Grant Awards Table
- Worksheets
    - Estimate Your Net Price
    - Financial Aid Comparison
    - Testing Fees and Budgeting
    - Application Expenses

Direct links to financial aid information and downloadable worksheets are available at https://collegeadmissionshq.org/PayLessForCollegeResources/

Links

Federal Student Aid

	Website
General Information	https://studentaid.gov
FSA-ID	https://fsaid.ed.gov
FAFSA	https://studentaid.gov/h/apply-for-aid/fafsa
Federal Student Aid Estimator (formally FAFSA4caster)	https://studentaid.gov/aid-estimator/
FAFSA Help	https://studentaid.gov/apply-for-aid/fafsa/filling-out/help
MyStudentAid App	https://studentaid.gov/mystudentaid-mobile-app
EFC Formula Guide	https://fsapartners.ed.gov/sites/default/files/2021-08/2223EFCFormulaGuide.pdf
Federal Grants	
PELL Grant	https://studentaid.gov/understand-aid/types/grants/pell
PELL Awards Table	https://fsapartners.ed.gov/sites/default/files/attachments/2021-01/20212022PellPaymentSchedule.pdf
FSEOG	https://studentaid.gov/understand-aid/types/grants/fseog
IASG	https://studentaid.gov/understand-aid/types/grants/iraq-afghanistan-service
TEACH Grant	https://studentaid.gov/understand-aid/types/grants/teach
Federal Loans	
Direct	https://studentaid.gov/understand-aid/types/loans/subsidized-unsubsidized
PLUS	https://studentaid.gov/understand-aid/types/loans/plus
Work-Study	
Work-Study	https://studentaid.gov/understand-aid/types/work-study
FAFSA Simplification ACT	
Full text	https://drive.google.com/file/d/1NdNqw64sCTWZrp7KWKLkey_cLC_ztfqH/view?usp=sharing

A

State Student Aid

	Website
State Financial Aid Programs	https://nasfaa.org/State_Financial_Aid_Programs
State-Based College Grants	http://www.collegescholarships.org/grants/state.htm
State Loans	http://www.collegescholarships.org/loans/state.htm
State Deadlines to File FAFSA	https://studentaid.gov/apply-for-aid/fafsa/fafsa-deadlines
States' Rules for Positioning Colleges on the FAFSA	https://studentaid.ed.gov/sa/fafsa/filling-out/school-list

Aid for Military Service

	Website
ROTC	**General:** https://studentaid.gov/understand-aid/types/military - rotc-scholarships **Army:** www.goarmy.com/rotc.html **Air Force:** www.afrotc.com **Navy:** www.nrotc.navy.mil **Navy Marine option:** https://www.netc.navy.mil/Commands/Naval-Service-Training-Command/NROTC/Marine/
US Department of Veterans Affairs	https://www.va.gov/education/
IASG	https://studentaid.gov/understand-aid/types/grants/iraq-afghanistan-service
Scholarships	**American Legion:** https://www.legion.org/scholarships **AMVETS:** https://amvets.org/scholarships **Disabled American Veterans:** https://www.fastweb.com/directory/scholarships-for-disabled-veterans **Paralyzed Veterans of America:** https://pva.org/find-support/scholarship-program **Veterans of Foreign Wars:** https://www.vfw.org/assistance/student-veterans-support

Scholarship Databases

	Website
Fastweb	https://www.fastweb.com/college-scholarships
CareerOneStop	https://www.careeronestop.org/toolkit/training/find-scholarships.aspx
Petersons	https://www.petersons.com/scholarship-search
Unigo	https://unigo.com/scholarships
Chegg	https://chegg.com/scholarships
Niche	https://niche.com/colleges/scholarships
Scholarships.com	https://scholarships.com
College Board Scholarship Search	https://bigfuture.collegeboard.org/scholarship-search

Financial Aid Forms

	Website
FAFSA	https://studentaid.gov/h/apply-for-aid/fafsa
FSA ID	https://fsaid.ed.gov
FAFSA Instructions	https://studentaid.gov/apply-for-aid/fafsa/filling-out
CSS Profile	https://cssprofile.collegeboard.org
Schools that require the CSS Profile	https://profile.collegeboard.org/profile/ppi/participatinginstitutions.aspx
Institutional	Refer to the college's financial aid page

College Information

	Website
College Navigator	https://nces.ed.gov/collegenavigator/
U.S.News Best Colleges	https://www.usnews.com/best-colleges
Graduation Rates	https://nces.ed.gov/collegenavigator/ Enter college name; then look under "Retention and Graduation Rates" http://www.collegeresults.org/ Click "Compare Colleges." Enter colleges of interest, then click "Retention and Progression Rates"
College Endowments	https://drive.google.com/file/d/1ATTT1lWAI3m4YeZpIq9sGF7FF3xYj2yw/view?usp=sharing

Average Percent Need Met/Percentage of Students with 100% Need Met

	Website
U.S.News Best Colleges	https://www.usnews.com/best-colleges Search for the college, then look under "Tuition and Financial Aid"
Common Data Set	Internet search the college name and "Common Data Set" Information is found in Section H of the college's CDS
Ask the College	Call the college's financial aid office

Education Loan Information

	Website
Federal Direct Loans	https://studentaid.ed.gov/sa/types/loans/subsidized-unsubsidized
Federal PLUS Loans	https://studentaid.gov/understand-aid/types/loans/plus
State Loans	http://www.collegescholarships.org/loans/state.htm
Student Loan Calculators	https://studentloanhero.com/calculators/

Rent/Buy Textbooks Online

	Website
Textbooks	https://www.chegg.com https://www.amazon.com/New-Used-Textbooks-Books/b?ie=UTF8&node=465600 https://www.valorebooks.com https://www.campusbooks.com/
StudentRate	https://www.studentrate.com

Study Abroad Information

	Website
Federal Aid Abroad	https://studentaid.gov/understand-aid/types/international
Cost of Living Abroad	https://www.expatistan.com/cost-of-living
World University Rankings	https://www.timeshighereducation.com/world-university-rankings https://www.topuniversities.com/qs-world-university-rankings

Guide to the Common Data Set

There are many sources of college data on the internet, but the most comprehensive information can be found in the college's most recent Common Data Set. The Common Data Set form was created by the college data compilers, College Board, Peterson's, and U.S. News & World Report, to make accurate and relevant college data available to students, parents, counselors, and others interested in higher education. Participating* colleges supply data about their institutions each year, which is then compiled into an easy-to-read format. You can find a college's Common Data Set on the college's website, through an Internet search, or by asking the college admissions officers to supply it. A college's Common Data Set is divided into ten sections that provide the following information:

A. **General Information**—address, type of school, degrees offered, contact information

B. **Enrollment and Persistence**—number of students and the gender/race/ethnic makeup of the student body; four, five, and six-year graduation rates; freshman retention rates

C. **First-Time, First-Year (Freshman) Admission**--acceptance rate, admission requirements, SAT/ACT mid- 50% for previous year's class, tests used for admission and placement, application fees, class rank data of previous year's class, deferment options, GPA statistics of previous year's class, Early Decision and Early Action data from previous year's class

D. **Transfer Admission**—acceptance rates, admissions criteria, transfer credit policies

E. **Academic Offerings and Policies**—special study options such as distance learning, double major, honors programs, student designed major, study abroad, etc.; general education requirements

F. **Student Life**—percentage of students from out-of-state, Greek Life statistics, activities offered, ROTC information, housing options

G. **Annual Expenses**—tuition and fees, room and board; estimated costs of books, supplies, transportation, and personal expenses; minimum and maximum credits allowed each semester; per-credit tuition

H. **Financial Aid**—total federal and college grant and scholarship awards; total student loan and work study amounts; total parent loans amounts; total athletic scholarships amounts; numbers of students applying for and getting financial aid; percent need met; average need-based award; number of students receiving non-need-based (merit) aid; financial aid forms required; types of need-based and merit aid awarded

I. **Instructional Faculty and Class Size**—percent full-time faculty, diversity of faculty body, student:faculty ratio, percentage of classes with less than 10, 20, 30, 40, 50, and 100 students

J. **Degrees Conferred**—a full listing of all majors offered, and the numbers and types of degrees awarded in each

**If a college does not participate in the CDS program, some CDS information can also be found on the government's College Navigator website. The student must call the college to get information not found on the Navigator site, such as important financial aid statistics, some admissions and student life information, faculty information, and class size statistics.*

© 2021 College Admissions HQ

2021-22 Pell Grant Awards Table

EFC	Enrollment Status				EFC	Enrollment Status			
(Expected Family Contribution)	Full Time	¾ Time	½ Time	< ½ Time	(Expected Family Contribution)	Full Time	¾ Time	½ Time	< ½ Time
0	$6,495	$4,871	$3,248	$1,624	2901-3000	$3,545	$2,659	$1,773	$886
1-100	$6,445	$4,834	$3,223	$1,611	3001-3100	$3,445	$2,584	$1,723	$861
101-200	$6,345	$4,759	$3,173	$1,586	3101-3200	$3,345	$2,509	$1,673	$836
201-300	$6,245	$4,684	$3,123	$1,561	3201-3300	$3,245	$2,434	$1,623	$811
301-400	$6,145	$4,609	$3,073	$1,536	3301-3400	$3,145	$2,359	$1,573	$786
401-500	$6,045	$4,534	$3,023	$1,511	3401-3500	$3,045	$2,284	$1,523	$761
501-600	$5,945	$4,459	$2,973	$1,486	3501-3600	$2,945	$2,209	$1,473	$736
601-700	$5,845	$4,384	$2,923	$1,461	3601-3700	$2,845	$2,134	$1,423	$711
701-800	$5,745	$4,309	$2,873	$1,436	3701-3800	$2,745	$2,059	$1,373	$686
801-900	$5,645	$4,234	$2,823	$1,411	3801-3900	$2,645	$1,984	$1,323	$661
901-1000	$5,545	$4,159	$2,773	$1,386	3901-4000	$2,545	$1,909	$1,273	0
1001-1100	$5,445	$4,084	$2,723	$1,361	4001-4100	$2,445	$1,834	$1,223	0
1101-1200	$5,345	$4,009	$2,673	$1,336	4101-4200	$2,345	$1,759	$1,173	0
1201-1300	$5,295	$3,934	$2,623	$1,311	4201-4300	$2,245	$1,684	$1,123	0
1301-1400	$5,145	$3,859	$2,573	$1,286	4301-4400	$2,145	$1,609	$1,073	0
1401-1500	$5,045	$3,784	$2,523	$1,261	4401-4500	$2,045	$1,534	$1,023	0
1501-1600	$4,945	$3,709	$2,473	$1,236	4501-4600	$1,945	$1,459	$973	0
1601-1700	$4,845	$3,634	$2,423	$1,211	4601-4700	$1,845	$1,384	$923	0
1701-1800	$4,745	$3,559	$2,373	$1,186	4701-4800	$1,745	$1,309	$873	0
1801-1900	$4,645	$3,484	$2,323	$1,161	4801-4900	$1,645	$1,234	$823	0
1901-2000	$4,545	$3,409	$2,273	$1,136	4901-5000	$1,545	$1,159	$723	0
2001-2100	$4,445	$3,334	$2,223	$1,111	5001-5100	$1,445	$1,084	$673	0
2101-2200	$4,345	$3,259	$2,173	$1,086	5101-5200	$1,345	$1,009	0	0
2201-2300	$4,245	$3,184	$2,123	$1,061	5201-5300	$1,245	$934	0	0
2301-2400	$4,145	$3,109	$2,073	$1,036	5301-5400	$1,145	$859	0	0
2401-2500	$4,045	$3,034	$2,023	$1,011	5401-5500	$1.045	$784	0	0
2501-2600	$3,945	$2,959	$1,973	$986	5501-5600	$945	$709	0	0
2601-2700	$3,845	$2,884	$1,923	$961	5601-5700	$845	0	0	0
2701-2800	$3,745	$2,809	$1,873	$836	5701-5800	$742	0	0	0
2801-2900	$3,645	$2,734	$1,823	$911	5801-5846	$672	0	0	0
					5847 +	0	0	0	0

Pell Grant awards listed here refer to colleges with a Cost of Attendance (COA) greater than $6,495. For lower COAs follow the link to the full 2021-22 Pell Grant Awards Table in the Links section of Appendix A. Pell Grant awards for 2022-23 school year will be released in January 2022.

© 2021 College Admissions HQ

ESTIMATE YOUR NET PRICE WORKSHEET

Your Estimated EFC ______________ *(use the online EFC calculator,* FAFSA4caster*)*

COLLEGE			
COA *Direct and Indirect costs*			
Your Estimated Need *COA - EFC*			
Average % Need Met *See Appendix A for links to this information*			
Estimated Dollar Amount of Need the College will Meet *(avg. % Need met) X (your Need)*			
Scholarships You Are Likely to Get *From the college or an outside organization*			
Total Federal and State Grants You Are Likely to Get			
Total Federal and State Loans You Are Likely to Get *Freshman Fed Direct Loan = $5,500*			
Federal Work-Study *Averages $2,000*			
Remaining Need *(your Need) – (gov. aid + scholarships)*			
Likely College Grant *(estimated dollar amount of Need the college will meet) – (remaining Need)*			
GAP *(your estimated Need) – (all aid awarded)*			
Estimated NET PRICE *(COA) – (grants and scholarships)*			
Estimated Immediate Out-of-Pocket Costs *The amount you must pay when the college bill comes (EFC + GAP + Work-Study)*			
Calculate Your Costs Without a Scholarship			
Adjusted Remaining Need *(your Need) – (government aid)*			
Likely College Grant *(est. dollar amount of Need the college will meet) –(adjusted remaining Need)*			
ADJUSTED Estimated NET PRICE *(COA) – (government and college grants)*			
Estimated Immediate Out-of-Pocket Costs *The amount you must pay when the college bill comes (EFC + GAP + Work-Study)*			

© 2021 College Admissions HQ

FINANCIAL AID COMPARISON WORKSHEET

		College			
COA	Direct Costs:	Tuition and Fees			
		Room and Board			
	Indirect Costs:	Books and Supplies			
		Personal Expenses			
Total COA (Direct + Indirect Costs)					
		EFC			
		Need (COA – EFC)			
Gift Aid		Federal Grants (Pell, FSEOG, TEACH, IASG)			
		College Grant			
		State Grant			
		College Scholarship			
		Outside Gift Aid (Tuition Benefits, Outside Scholarships)			
		Total Gift Aid			
NET PRICE (COA – Total Gift Aid)					
Self-Help Aid		Federal Work-Study			
		Federal Direct Subsidized Loan			
		Fed Direct Unsubsidized Loan			
		State Loan			
		Total Self-Help Aid			
GAP (Need – Gift Aid – Self-Help Aid)					
Immediate Out-of-Pocket Costs The amount you must pay when the college bill comes (EFC + GAP + Work-Study)					

© 2021 College Admissions HQ

A

2021-22 TESTING FEES AND BUDGETING WORKSHEET

Test Name	Testing Fee	Change Test Date Fee	Late Registration Fee	Free Reports	Score Report Fee	Rush/Prior Reports	BUDGET	
							Number of Schools	TOTAL
SAT	$55	$25	$30	4	$12	$31		
ACT	$60	$40	$36	4	$16	$39		
ACT with Writing	$85	$40	$36	4	$16	$39		
AP	$96		$40	1	$15	$25		
CLEP	$89 + Test center admin fees			1	$20.00			
Total Cost of Testing								

**After June 2021, the College Board will no longer offer SAT Subject Tests or the optional SAT Essay.*

© 2021 College Admissions HQ

APPLICATION EXPENSES WORKSHEET

College			
Application Fee			
Required Tests/Fees			
Recommended Tests/Fees			
Score Report Fees			
Transcript Fees			
Campus Visits *hotels, food, transportation*			
Postage *Mailing costs for supplemental materials and/or letters of recommendation*			
TOTAL COST			

© 2021 College Admissions HQ

A

GUIDE TO THE FAFSA

- What Is the FAFSA?
- Why File a FAFSA?
- How to Access the FAFSA
- What You Need to Fill Out the FAFSA
- The Six Sections of the FAFSA
- Other Important Things to Know About the FAFSA

What Is the FAFSA?

The FAFSA, Free Application for Federal Student Aid, is the primary financial aid form used to access college financial aid.

The purpose of the FAFSA is to analyze student and parent income and assets to arrive at the family's EFC (Expected Family Contribution), and to determine your eligibility for federal grants, loans, and Work-Study. Appendix D is a full guide to how your EFC is determined.

Students must file a new FAFSA each year to access financial aid. A new FAFSA is released on Oct 1 for the following school year.

SEE CHAPTER EIGHT

The FAFSA information in this Appendix is fully updated for the 2022-23 school year. However, many changes to the FAFSA will be phased in over the 2023-24 and 2024-25 school years.

Why File a FAFSA?

In order to access any need-based aid, you must file a FAFSA. If you have financial Need, (i.e. your EFC is less than the COA of the school), you qualify for need-based aid (federal, state, and college grants, Federal Direct Student Loans, state student loans, and Work-Study).

To access Federal Direct Student Loans or parent PLUS loans, you must file a FAFSA even if you have no financial need.

To access student federal aid for military families (including grants, scholarships, and federal loans), you must file a FAFSA, even if you have no financial need.

Many states require you to file a FAFSA and use it to determine your eligibility for state student aid (grants and student loans).

Colleges require your FAFSA information to examine your finances, EFC, and eligibility for federal aid. With this information, they determine the makeup of your entire financial aid package, including how much college grant money they will award you. You may also be required to file a FAFSA to apply for some college scholarships, even if you have no financial need.

How to Access the FAFSA

The FAFSA is an online form, released each year on Oct 1, and found at www.FAFSA.gov or accessed through the MyStudentAid app.

You have the option to file a paper version of the FAFSA (available as a download from the FAFSA website), but it is far better to file electronically. The electronic form is processed faster, catches errors before you've submitted, and uses "skip-logic" to skip questions not relevant to you, making it much shorter than the paper version.

Be sure to go to the correct website, which looks like this:

What You Need to Complete the FAFSA

1. An FSA ID

   Before you begin your FAFSA, you and one or both parents (if you are a dependent student) are strongly advised to get a Federal Student Aid ID, or FSA ID. The FSA ID will allow you to access and make changes to your FAFSA online and to sign your FAFSA electronically. The FSA ID also gives you access to all your student aid information and to the National Student Loan Database System (NSLDS) to keep track of all your federal student loans.

   To create your FSA ID, you will fill out a simple form including your name, date of birth, social security number, a valid email address and to create a username, password, and security questions.

   Your FSA ID will be verified through your email, can be used immediately, and will not expire.

2. Social Security Numbers for Student and Parents (if you are a dependent student)
3. Financial Information for Student and Parents (if you are a dependent student):
   - W-2 and tax forms from TWO years prior to the year you plan to enter college (e.g. a student entering college in 2022 will use income information from parents' and student's 2020 tax forms)
   - Untaxed Income Information:
     - Contributions to retirement accounts
     - IRA deductions and other qualified plans
     - Child support received
     - Tax-exempt interest income
     - Untaxed portions of IRA distributions and pensions
     - Untaxed portions of Health Savings Accounts
     - Military Benefits: Housing, food, and other living allowances (excluding the value of on-base military housing or basic military allowance for housing)
     - Clergy benefits: Housing, food, and other allowances
     - Veterans non-education benefits: Disability, Death Pension, Dependency & Indemnity Compensation (DIC), and/or VA Educational Work-Study allowances
     - Other untaxed benefits: worker's compensation, disability, untaxed foreign income, etc.
     - Money received on the student's behalf (cash, gifts, loans, tuition payments, bills paid, etc.) by anyone other than the custodial parent(s) (exclude financial support that is part of a legal child support agreement)
     - Distributions to the student beneficiary from a 529 plan that is owned by someone other than the student or parents

     DO NOT include the following untaxed income on the FAFSA:

     Foster care benefits and extended foster care benefits, adoption payments, student aid, earned income credit, additional child tax credit, IRA and pension rollovers, welfare payments, untaxed

B

Social Security benefits, Supplemental Security Income, Workforce Innovation and Opportunity Act education benefits, combat pay, benefits from flexible spending programs, foreign income exclusion, federal tax credit for special fuels

- Additional Required Financial Information

    - Education tax credits (American Opportunity Tax Credit and Lifetime Learning Tax Credit) you received in the reporting year

    - Child support paid because of divorce or separation or as a result of a legal requirement (don't include support for children in parents' household)

    - Parent and student taxable earnings from need-based employment such as Work-Study, fellowships, assistantships

    - Parent and student *taxable* college grant and scholarships reported to IRS as income *(Usually a scholarship or grant is tax free as long as you are a degree candidate and the award is used to pay for tuition and required fees, books, supplies and equipment. There are some scholarship and grants that are not tax exempt.)*

    - Taxable portion of combat pay or special combat pay that was included in parents' adjusted gross income (don't include untaxed combat pay)

    - Earnings from cooperative education programs offered by a college

- Asset Information for Student and Parents (if you are a dependent student)

    - Total balance of cash, savings, and checking accounts as of the day you file the FAFSA

    - Net value of investments as of the day you file the FAFSA—CDs, money market funds, mutual funds, stocks and stock options, bonds, other securities, real estate (other than your primary residence), rental property, other property investments, commodities, trust funds, education savings accounts (529s, Coverdell, prepaid tuition plans). Dependent students report Education Savings Accounts (ESAs) as parent assets

    - Uniform Transfers to Minors Act (UTMA) or Uniform Gifts to Minors Act (UGMA) accounts owned by the student

    DO NOT include the following assets on the FAFSA:

    The home in which you live, the value of your life insurance, retirement plans (401k, pension funds, annuities, non-education IRAs, Keogh plans, etc.) and UTMA or UGMA accounts for which parents are the custodians and not the owner

- Business Financial Information for Student and Parents (if dependent)

  Report net value of a business or farm owned by the student or parents (Family businesses and small businesses with fewer than 100 employees are exempt. Family farms that the student and/or parents live on and operate are also exempt)

4. List of colleges you want to receive your FAFSA information

The Six Sections of the FAFSA

1. Student Demographics: Enter your name, date of birth, social security number, address, and other basic information.

   The name on the FAFSA MUST exactly match the name on your social security card or your FAFSA will be delayed.

2. School Selection: Enter a list of colleges to which you plan to apply.

   Enter the name and address of the school or its federal code.

   You are allowed to enter up to ten schools at a time on the online FAFSA. If you are applying to more than ten schools, fill in the first ten, complete the FAFSA and submit. After you receive your student aid report, or SAR, log back in and click "Make FAFSA Corrections." Remove some or all of the first ten schools, add the new schools, and resubmit. The first ten schools will still get your FAFSA information. However, if you make any changes to your original FAFSA information after adding new schools, only the currently listed schools will receive the new information. In this case, contact the first set of schools and submit the changes directly to them.

   If you are applying for financial aid at public colleges in your home state, your state may require that you list their schools in order of preference or at the top of the list. See Appendix A for a link to your state's rules for FAFSA positioning of state schools on your list.

3. Dependency Status: Here you answer a series of YES/NO questions to determine your dependency status. You are considered an INDEPENDENT student in the college financial aid analysis only if you are one of the following:

   - 24 years old or older
   - Married (or separated, but not divorced)

- A graduate or professional student
- Providing more than half the financial support for your child(ren) or other dependents
- An orphan, in foster care, or a ward of the court
- In legal guardianship or an emancipated minor
- Homeless (or at risk of being homeless)
- Currently serving in the Armed Forces or a veteran of the Armed Forces

If you are considered a dependent student and your parents refuse to give you their financial information, you may not be able to receive federal aid or get an EFC. However, the FAFSA gives detailed instructions on how to proceed without parent financial information, so it's important to file anyway. You must also check with the colleges themselves to discuss how they will assess your finances without parent information.

4. <u>Parent Demographics</u>: Enter parent(s) or step-parent names, dates of birth, social security numbers, household size, education level, and how many children in the household will be attending college that year.

   If you are a dependent student and your parents are divorced, separated, unmarried, or remarried, see Appendix E for detailed information on how to report parent information on the FAFSA.

5. <u>Financial Information</u>: Provide both parent (if you are a dependent student) and student income and assets. You will supply income information from TWO years before the year you plan to enter college (prior-prior year). For example, if you plan to enter college in 2022, enter income information from your 2020 tax forms. Most families will have filed their taxes for the requested year and can use the FAFSA's Data Retrieval Tool (DRT) to import all IRS income information directly into their FAFSA.

   To access the DRT, click "already completed my taxes." Then click, "Link to the IRS." Log in to the DTR with your FSA ID, enter your information, and click "Transfer My Tax Information into the FAFSA Form." You will know which tax questions have been filled in on your FAFSA because the answer fields will say "Transferred from the IRS."

   In order to use the DRT on the FAFSA, parent(s) and students must:

   - have a valid Social Security number
   - have an FSA ID

- ◦ if married, not have filed as "married filing separately" or "head of household"
- ◦ not have filed an amended federal income tax return for the reported year
- ◦ not have filed a foreign income tax return instead of, or in addition to, the U.S. federal income tax return

In addition to your income information, you must list your and your parents' reportable assets. Enter the current net value of assets as of the day you file your FAFSA. (See above for a full list of reportable and excluded assets).

The 2022-23 FAFSA allows a small asset protection allowance to married or remarried parents and to unmarried legal parents who live together. Married students also get a small asset protection allowance.

There is no 2022-23 asset protection allowance for dependent students, unmarried independent students, or single parents.

Dependent students whose parents' annual income is less than $50,000 and who meet certain other criteria (see the Appendix D for details), qualify for the simplified needs test and do not have to report either parent or student assets on the FAFSA for federal aid. This is dependent only on parent income regardless of the student's income and assets. However, certain states do require you to report assets to determine eligibility for state aid.

Dependent students whose parents' annual income is less than $27,000 and who meet certain other criteria (see the Appendix D for details), qualify for an automatic EFC (Expected Family Contribution) of ZERO. This is dependent only on parent income regardless of the student's income and assets.

6. <u>Sign and Submit</u>: The last section of the FAFSA is where you and one of your parents sign the application with your FSA IDs and submit. Don't submit your FAFSA until you have fully checked your entries. Errors on your FAFSA will delay its processing—sometimes by weeks, which may cost you some financial aid. If you don't want to sign electronically, you have the option to print out a signature page and mail it separately, but choosing this option will significantly delay the processing of your FAFSA.

   Once you submit your completed FAFSA online, you will receive an email shortly thereafter which will give you your EFC. Your Student Aid Report, or SAR, will be emailed to you within 24 hours. The SAR contains all the information you entered into the FAFSA and is the document your schools will receive. The SAR also includes your EFC and your eligibility for federal grants and Direct student loans.

GOOD TO KNOW

The SAR will also indicate whether or not you've been selected for verification. FAFSA verification is a process used to confirm that the data you've entered into the FAFSA is correct. Most colleges verify 30% of submitted FAFSAs and some schools verify all of them. If your FAFSA is incomplete, it will automatically be flagged for verification—usually just to get the missing information. If data on the FAFSA is contradictory, or you repeatedly amend your FAFSA, you may also be flagged.

If you are selected for verification, don't panic. Fix your mistakes or omissions immediately and resubmit your amended FAFSA as fast as you can. It can take 2-3 weeks to verify your FAFSA, which may delay the allocation of financial aid to you.

Other Important Things to Know About the FAFSA

- Be accurate when filing a FAFSA. If you make a mistake, you may lose any aid you were awarded based on incorrect information and you may have to pay it back, with penalties. And never lie about your income or assets – it is a form of fraud punishable by fines up to $20,000 and possibly prison.
- You must file a new FAFSA each year you apply for need-based financial aid.
- At many colleges, the deadline to submit the FAFSA is late January or early February for incoming freshmen applying Regular Decision, but deadlines vary widely from college to college. It is *critical* to submit the FAFSA by the college's deadline. If you are filing Early Decision, the deadline will be earlier.
- Be certain to also meet your state's deadline for filing the FAFSA each year. States award their monies early, and late filers may miss out completely. The FAFSA homepage offers a link to check the deadline in your state.
- The FAFSA takes about 30-45 minutes to fill out if you have all your financial information on hand.
- You are permitted to log in and out of your account to make changes as many times as you want before you submit your final version. After submitting, you are permitted to amend your FAFSA if you've discovered mistakes or want to add new colleges. However, don't amend too many times or your FAFSA will be flagged for verification, which may delay its processing.

GUIDE TO THE CSS PROFILE

- What Is the CSS Profile?
- Why Some Colleges Require the CSS Profile
- How to Access the CSS Profile
- What You Need to Complete the CSS Profile
- The Sixteen Sections of the CSS Profile
- The FAFSA vs the CSS Profile
- Other Important Things to Know About the CSS Profile
- Colleges and Programs That Require the CSS Profile

What Is the CSS Profile?

The CSS Profile (College Scholarship Service Profile) is a financial aid form created and administered by the College Board and used by approximately 240 US colleges, universities, professional schools, and scholarship programs to award more than $9 billion in non-government grants and scholarships (free money) to students. Colleges that require the CSS Profile are typically the most expensive and competitive colleges and often award individuals very large need-based grants.

Colleges that require the CSS Profile almost always also require the FAFSA (which determines your eligibility for federal and state aid).

Unlike the FAFSA, which is free for all students to file, the CSS Profile is free only if the student's family has an adjusted gross income less than $100,000, or the student qualified for an SAT fee waiver, or the student is an orphan or ward of the court under age 24.

For all other students, the CSS Profile costs $25 to file for the first college and $16 for each additional college.

Why Some Colleges Require the CSS Profile

The CSS Profile asks many more questions about your finances than the FAFSA does, which gives the college a better sense of your ability to pay before deciding how much of their own grant money they will award you. Each college can add even more probing questions in the supplements section. These colleges want to know if your family has financial resources not revealed by the FAFSA.

With the additional information about your finances the college may decide that your financial need is lower and your EFC higher than what the FAFSA has determined, in which case they will give you less need-based aid.

However, the CSS Profile can also work in your favor. Because it considers certain kinds of parent expenses not asked about on the FAFSA (high medical and dental expenses, siblings' secondary education tuition, care costs of an elderly family member, underwater mortgages, and other financial hardships), the college may determine you have a *lower* EFC than the FAFSA has determined and award you more need-based aid.

C

How to Access the CSS Profile

The CSS Profile is an online form, released each year on Oct 1, and found on the College Board's website, https://cssprofile.collegeboard.org/.

You must create a College Board Account to access the CSS Profile. You may already have a College Board account if you have signed up for or taken the PSAT, SAT, or AP exam.

What You Need to Complete the CSS Profile

- A College Board Account
- All the information needed for the FAFSA (see Appendix B)
- Contact information for non-custodial parents
- Value of Parents' tax-deferred retirement, pension, annuity, and savings plans
- Additional Medicare tax paid
- Total amount of parents' itemized deductions
- Value of parents' flexible spending accounts for medical expenses and dependent care expenses
- Amount of wages withheld for parents' Health Savings Account(s)
- Amount of foreign income exclusion reported to IRS
- Amount of cash gifts to parents or any money paid on their behalf
- Information about parents' income and benefits from the current year (in addition to prior-prior year income information required by the FAFSA)
- Expected parent income and benefits for the next year, including expected cash gifts
- Current market value of parents' home
- Net value of Parents' assets (as of the day you file), including cash, stocks, bonds, savings bonds, mutual funds, money market funds, certificates of deposit, 529 college savings or pre-paid tuition plans, other college savings plans, non-qualified (non-retirement) annuities, trust funds, commodities, precious & strategic metals, installment & land sale contracts (including seller-financed mortgages), and other valuables (jewelry, artwork, precious metals, antiques), other real estate
- Parent business or farm details
- Value of parent assets held in names of siblings of student

- Parent educational loan payments
- Parent medical and dental expenses including premiums (and estimated payments for following year)
- Amount of elementary, junior high, and high school tuition for dependent children paid by parents (and estimated payments for following year)
- Parents' monthly mortgage payment
- Amount of scholarship, grants, or gift aid the student received the previous year
- Amount of money parents paid toward student's college costs the previous year
- Value of trusts of which the student is a beneficiary
- Cost of college of any sibling also attending college that year
- Amount parents will pay toward sibling college costs that year

Additional financial information may be asked in supplemental questions required by individual colleges.

The Sixteen Sections of the CSS Profile

1. Getting Started: Enter your name, address, date of birth, social security number, email, phone number, marital status, citizenship status, year in college, and dependency status.
2. Parent Information: Enter names of parents (including biological, adoptive, step-parents, legal guardians), marital status, and living arrangements.
3. Residence: Enter the country and zip code of your residence.
4. Academic Information: Enter your current school year, high school name and location, and list of colleges or programs you wish to receive your CSS Profile application.
5. Parent Details: Enter each parent's name, date of birth, social security number, address, contact information, education level, occupation, employer, types and current value of existing retirement plans.
6. Parent Income: Enter parents' federal income tax information for two years prior to the year you will attend college, untaxed income information (HSA or FSA contributions from both parents and employers, benefits information, money gifted to parents or paid on their behalf), parent taxed

C

and untaxed income and benefits from current year, expected parent taxed and untaxed income and benefits for the year you will be attending college.

7. Child Support: Enter any child support paid to another household or received from another household two years prior to the year you attend college and the current year.

8. Housing Information: Provide details on where you and your family live, including address, ownership status (own or rent), monthly housing payment, home purchase year, price, current market value, debt owed on mortgage, and student housing information if you do not live at home with your parents.

9. Parent Assets: List the net value of all parent assets including cash, stocks, bonds, savings bonds, mutual funds, money market funds, certificates of deposit, 529 college savings or pre-paid tuition plans, other college savings plans, non-qualified (non-retirement) annuities, trust funds, commodities, precious & strategic metals, installment & land sale contracts (including seller-financed mortgages), other valuables (jewelry, artwork, precious metals, antiques), other real estate, businesses and farms, and assets held in the names of their children.

10. Parent Expenses: Include all expenses incurred prior-prior year and current year -- medical/dental expenses, education loan debt (including student, parent, and sibling debt), alimony, living expenses (utilities, food, clothing, car expenses, insurance, etc.).

11. Household Summary: Include names, ages, and relationship of all members of the student's parents' household who receive more than half their support from them.

12. Student Income: Enter student's federal income tax information for two years prior to the year you will attend college and the current year, untaxed income information, tax form filed, tax filing status, gifts given to the student by anyone other than the parents, student expected income for the next year, student resources (money you expect to receive to help with college costs from your parents, other relatives, scholarships and grants from sources other than the college to which you're applying, employer tuition benefits).

13. Student Assets: Enter information about different kinds of assets that belong to you including investments (stocks & stock options, bonds, savings bonds, mutual funds, money market funds, Uniform Gifts to Minors (or similar accounts), certificates of deposit, non-qualified (non-retirement) annuities, commodities, precious & strategic metals, and installment & land sale contracts (including seller-financed mortgages), trusts, retirement assets,

real estate, etc. Provide the value of these assets as of the day you submit the CSS Profile.

14. Special Circumstances: Here you are given the opportunity to discuss nuances in your finances, such as uneven income year to year, loss of a job, exceptional medical or dental expenses, siblings in private school, catastrophic events or natural disasters, eldercare expenses or financial support of other family members, financial hardship due to the Covid-19 pandemic or any other aspect of your finances that you want to include to help demonstrate a difficulty to pay college costs.
15. Supplemental Questions: Each college you apply to may request that you answer additional questions about your finances.
16. Sign and Submit: Here you sign and submit your application electronically. If information is missing in any section, you will be asked to return to the section and enter the missing information. You will be given the chance to review your entire application before submitting.

The FAFSA vs the CSS Profile

	FAFSA	**CSS Profile**
General Information		
Administrator	US Department of Education	College Board
Cost to File	Free	Free for undergraduate students if: • Family adjusted gross income is under $100,000 • The student qualified for an SAT fee waiver • The student is an orphan or ward of the court under the age of 24 For all other students: $25 for the first application; $16 for each additional college
Type of Aid	Federal, State, and Institutional	Institutional

Treatment of Income		
Automatic Zero EFC	Parent income below $27,000+	None
Minimum Student Contribution	None	$3,000-$6,000/year
Cost of Living (COL) Expenses	State tax allowances included	Considers regional differences in COL expenses
Income Allowances	Income protection, income tax, employment expense allowances included	Income protection, income tax, employment expense, K-12 tuition, medical/dental expense, annual college savings allowances included
Special Circumstances	Excluded	Considers special circumstances that may affect the family's ability to pay for college including impacts of COVID-19
Treatment of Assets		
Home Equity of Primary Residence	Excluded	Considered
Net Worth of Small Businesses++	Excluded+++	Considered
Student Assets	20% (no asset protection allowance)	25% (no asset protection allowance)
529 Plans	Only considers parent or student-owned plans	Considers all 529 plans that list the student as the beneficiary, regardless of who owns the plan
Sibling Assets	Excluded	Considers assets of siblings under age 19 and not in college
Parent Assets	Assessed at a maximum of 5.64% with a small asset protection allowance for married parents based on the older parent's age	Assessed at a maximum of 5% after an allowance for education savings and emergencies
Simplified Needs Test	Parent income below $50,000+ qualifies family for a simplified version of the FAFSA that excludes parent and student assets	Does not have a simplified needs test but will exclude some losses from AGI

Reporting when Divorced/Separated/Unmarried/Remarried		
Income and Assets of Non-Custodial Parent	Excluded	Considered
Income and Assets of Step-parent	Considered	Considered
Biological or Adoptive Parents Unmarried but Living Together	Considered	Considered
Effect of Having Multiple Children in College at the Same Time		
More than One Child Attending College at the Same Time	Parent contribution to the EFC is split evenly among them	Reduces parent contribution by 40% for each of 2 children, 55% for each of 3 children, 65% for each of 4 or more children in college at the same time

© 2021 College Admissions HQ

[+]Parents must have filed a 1040 without a Schedule 1 (unless the Schedule 1 was filed to report unemployment compensation, an Alaska Permanent Fund dividend, educator expenses, IRA deduction, or student loan interest deduction) OR not required to file any income tax return OR be a dislocated worker OR have anyone in the household receiving a federal means tested benefit within the last two years (see Appendix B for more details).

[++]Small Business is defined as having 100 or fewer full-time employees. Two half-time employees are counted as one full-time employee.

[+++]The family must own at least 51% of the business for it to be considered a family business and excluded from the EFC formula

Other Important Things to Know About the CSS Profile

- Like the online form of the FAFSA, the CSS Profile uses skip-logic to adapt the questions to the student's situation, so not all questions will appear to all students.
- You are permitted to log in and out of the CSS Profile as many times as you like before submitting your final version. Once submitted, you can make corrections only one time. If you need to make additional corrections, you must contact each school separately. You are permitted to add additional schools at any point.
- Deadlines for submissions vary between colleges. Be certain to submit your application no later than two weeks before the earliest priority filing date listed by the college.
- The CSS Profile is mostly about parent financial information. If you are a dependent student and your parents refuse to fill out the Profile, call the college and ask what you can do. Each college will have its own procedures.

2022-23 Colleges and Programs That Require the CSS Profile

Alabama A&M University
American University
Amherst College
Armenian Student Assoc of Amer
Babson College
Bard College
Bard College at Simons Rock
Barnard College
Bates College
Baylor University
Bennington College
Bentley U: McCallum Graduate
Bentley University
Berklee College of Music
Berry College
Birmingham-Southern College
Boston College
Boston U: School of Medicine
Boston University
Bowdoin College
Boyce College
Brandeis University
Brown University
Bryn Mawr College
Bucknell University
Buttonwood Foundation
California Institute of Tech
Carleton College
Carnegie Mellon University
Caroline E. Hill Scholar Fund
Case Western Reserve U: MED
Case Western Reserve University
Christendom College, VA
Claremont McKenna College
Clark University
Cleveland Institute of Music
Colby College
Colgate University
College of the Holy Cross
College of William and Mary
College of Wooster
Colorado College
Columbia U: Business School
Columbia U: College and Engineering
Columbia U: College of Dental Medicine
Columbia U: Occupational Therapy
Columbia U: School of Arts
Columbia U: School of General Studies, NY.
Columbia U: School of Law
Columbia U: Vagelos College of Physicians/ Surgeons
Connecticut College
Cornell U: College of Vet Medicine
Cornell U: School of Law
Cornell University
Cottey College
Dartmouth College
Dartmouth College: Thayer Sch
Davidson College
Denison University
DePauw University
Dickinson College
Drexel University
Duke Kunshan University
Duke University
Duke University School of Nursing
Duke University: Nicholas School of Environment
Duke University: School of Medicine
Earlham College, IN.
Eastman School of Music: U of Rochester

C

Elon University
Emerson College
Emory U: School of Medicine
Emory University
Fairfield University
Fordham University
Francis Ouimet School Fund
Franklin and Marshall College
Furman University
Geisel School of Medicine at Dartmouth
George Washington U: Law School
George Washington U: Public Health, DC
George Washington University
Georgetown U: Law Center
Georgetown University
Georgetown University in Qatar
Georgia Institute of Technology
Gestalt Institute of Cleveland
Gettysburg College
Global Citizen Year
Grinnell College
Gustavus Adolphus College
Hamilton College (NY)
Hampshire College
Harvard College
Harvard U: Dental School
Harvard U: Harvard Medical School
Harvey Mudd College
Haverford College
Hillsdale College
Hobart and William Smith Coll
Horace Greeley Scholarship Fund
Icahn Sch of Med at Mt Sinai
Illinois Wesleyan University
Ithaca College
Jacksonville University
Jewish Theological Seminary of America, NY
Johns Hopkins Bloomberg School of Public Health, M
Johns Hopkins University
Johns Hopkins University School of Medicine
Johns Hopkins University: Peabody Conservatory
Juilliard School, The
Kamehameha Schools
Kenyon College
Kutztown University
Lafayette College
Lake Forest College
Lawrence University
Lehigh University
Loras College, IA.
Loyola University Maryland
Macalester College
Manhattan School of Music
Marian University
Marietta College
Marist College
Massachusetts Inst of Tech
McGill University
Menlo College, CA.
MES Fund, Inc.
Middlebury College
Montessori Inst of North Texas
Mount Holyoke College
National Merit School Corp
New Canaan HS School Foundation
New Saint Andrews College
New York University
Northeastern University
Northland College
Northwestern College
Northwestern University
Norwich University
Oberlin College
Occidental College
Olivet College
Oregon State University

Otis College of Art and Design
Patrick Henry College
Pitzer College
Pomona College
Principia College
Providence College
Queens University at Kingston
Reed College
Rensselaer Polytechnic Inst
Rhode Island School of Design
Rhodes College
Rice University
Ringling College of Art and Design
Sacred Heart University
Saint Louis University
San Francisco Conservatory of Music
Santa Clara University
Scripps College
Sewanee: The University of the South
SF Mainliner Scholarship Program
Siena College
Skidmore College
Smith College
Southern Baptist Theo Sem
Southern Methodist University
Springfield College, MA
St. Edwards University
St. Johns College (MD)
St. Johns College (NM)
St. Olaf College
Stanford U: Sch of Medicine
Stanford U: School of Law
Stanford University
Stetson University
Stevens Institute Technology
Stonehill College
Stratford University: Falls Church, VA
Swarthmore College
Syracuse University
Texas Christian University
The 200 Club of Morris County
The Minerva Schools at KGI
Thomas Aquinas College (CA/MA)
Thomas College
Trevecca Nazarene University, TN
Trinity College (CT)
Trinity University
Tufts University
Tulane University
Union College (NY)
Univ of California: San Francisco
Univ of Chicago
Univ of Denver
Univ of Massachusetts: Medical School
Univ of Miami
Univ of Michigan
Univ of North Carolina Chapel
Univ of Notre Dame
Univ of Penn: Law School
Univ of Penn: Perelman School of Med
Univ of Pennsylvania
Univ of Pittsburgh: School of Med
Univ of Richmond
Univ of Rochester
Univ of Rochester School of Med/Dent
Univ of Southern California (USC)
Univ of Toronto, Canada
Univ of Virginia
Vanderbilt U: School of Medicine
Vanderbilt University
Vassar College
Villanova University
Virginia Commonwealth U: School of Med
Wake Forest Sch of Medicine
Wake Forest University
Wartburg College
Washington and Lee University
Washington University: St. Louis

Weill Cornell Medical School

Wellesley College

Wesleyan University

Westminster College, UT

Whitman College

Whitworth University

William Jewell College

Williams College

Woodrow Wilson Grad School of Teaching + Learning

Worcester Polytechnic Institute

Yale U: Physicians Associate Program

Yale U: School of Art

Yale U: School of Drama

Yale U: School of Medicine

Yale University

GUIDE TO THE EFC

- What Is the EFC?
- How Is the EFC Used?
- How to Know Your EFC Before Submitting the FAFSA
- How the EFC Is Calculated
- Six Important Facts About How the EFC Is Calculated
- Four Factors That Can Have a Large Impact on the Size of Your EFC
- Other EFC Facts
- If I Calculate That My EFC Is Very High, Should I Still File a FAFSA?

Your EFC (Expected Family Contribution) is a critical piece of your college costs. To fully understand how financial aid works, you must learn what your EFC is and how it is calculated. This will allow you to take steps to minimize it.

Most families are surprised, and sometimes horrified, to discover what their EFC is because it seems a ridiculously high cost to pay each year. Although it may once have reflected what a family could reasonably pay in one year, today your EFC actually reflects what you can pay in the current year *plus* what you can borrow and pay over time. For this reason, your EFC can contribute heavily to your overall college debt.

SEE CHAPTER EIGHT

The EFC information presented in this chapter is relevant for the 2022-23 school year. However, the EFC will be replaced with a new assessment formula when the FAFSA changes are phased in between the 2023-24 and 2024-25 school years.

What Is the EFC?

As discussed in Chapter 4, your EFC is the *minimum* dollar amount your family is expected to pay for college each year unless:

1. Your EFC is greater than the COA (Cost of Attendance) at a school or
2. You receive merit aid (scholarship) that is larger than your financial need

In most cases, you will pay more than your EFC each year -- in cash, assets, or college loans as detailed in Chapter 3.

Your EFC is generated each year through an analysis of student (and parent if you are a dependent student and spouse if you are married) income and assets as reported on the FAFSA (Free Application for Federal Student Aid).

A very small number of colleges use an additional financial aid form, the CSS Profile. These colleges use the information in both forms to generate a different EFC using the Institutional Methodology. See Appendix C for a table listing the differences between these two methodologies.

How Is the EFC Used?

Your EFC is used by the federal and most state governments to determine if you qualify for federal (and state) grants, federal (and state) student loans, and Work-Study. The colleges use your EFC to determine your financial need at their school with this equation:

COA – EFC = Need

If your EFC is less than the college's COA, you qualify for need-based financial aid at that college. The lower your EFC, the more need-based aid you qualify for. The college then builds your financial aid package by meeting some portion of your need with federal, state, and college aid.

How to Know Your EFC Before Submitting the FAFSA

Many families don't know their EFC until *after* they submit the FAFSA. However, you can and should get an estimate every year in high school so you can plan for the costs you're likely to be responsible for at any college of interest (see Chapter 3 for more information).

The quickest way to get your FAFSA-generated EFC is to use the government's Federal Student Aid Estimator, a simple, free, anonymous online EFC calculator. If you enter accurate income and asset value numbers, the EFC generated will also be accurate.

How the EFC Is Calculated

The federal government releases a free online EFC Formula Guide early in September each year to help you determine your EFC for the following school year. See Appendix A for a link to this guide.

The EFC Formula Guide is a downloadable form and includes worksheets and tables for both dependent and independent students, independent students with dependents, and families with exceptional Need. This guide shows you clearly how the family's EFC is calculated.

Dependent full-time students (the majority of FAFSA filers) only need a few pages—the parent and student worksheets (pages 9 and 10) and the 7 tables from which to make your calculations (pages 25-29). Blank versions of 2022-23 parent and student worksheets for full-time dependent students (EFC Formula A) and the appropriate tables are included at the end of this appendix and also as downloadable pdfs at https://collegeadmissionshq.org/PayLessForCollegeResources/.

Use the worksheets that correspond to your family situation and work through the calculations with your own numbers to get a full understanding of how the formula will specifically affect *your* EFC.

To demonstrate how to use these worksheets, the following forms show how a fictional family of four from Ohio (2 parents and 2 dependent children; both parents working, married filing jointly) arrives at their EFC of $10,980 (see the student worksheet, line 51).

Given: **Family of Four, One Child Going to College**

Parent one: age 45, 2020 salary of $38,000

Parent two: age 44, 2020 salary of $32,000

Parent 2020 interest income = $2,000

Parent 2020 Untaxed Income:
Contribution to 401K = $3,000

Parent cash, savings, and checking = $5,000

Parent investments = $21,000

Student 2020 income = $3,500

Student untaxed income = $2,000 (gift from a relative)

Student cash, savings, and checking = $800

Student investments = $10,000 (savings bond)

2022–2023 EFC FORMULA A: DEPENDENT STUDENT

REGULAR WORKSHEET Page 1 **A**

PARENTS' INCOME IN 2020		
1. Parents' adjusted gross income (FAFSA/SAR #84) If negative, enter zero.		72,000
2. a. Parent 1 (father/mother/stepparent) income earned from work (FAFSA/SAR #86) 38,000		
2. b. Parent 2 (father/mother/stepparent) income earned from work (FAFSA/SAR #87) + 32,000		
Total parents' income earned from work	=	70,000
3. Taxable income (If tax filers, enter the amount from line 1 above. If non-tax filers, enter the amount from line 2.)*		72,000
4. Total untaxed income and benefits: (total of FAFSA/SAR #92a through 92h)	+	3,000
5. Taxable and untaxed income (sum of line 3 and line 4)	=	75,000
6. Total additional financial information (total of FAFSA/SAR #91a through 91f)	−	0
7. TOTAL INCOME (line 5 minus line 6) May be a negative number.	=	75,000

ALLOWANCES AGAINST PARENTS' INCOME		
8. 2020 U.S. income tax paid (FAFSA/SAR #85) (tax filers only) If negative, enter zero.		1,629
9. State and other tax allowance (Table 1) If negative, enter zero.	+	3,000
10. Parent 1 (father/mother/stepparent) Social Security tax allowance (Table 3)	+	2,907
11. Parent 2 (father/mother/stepparent) Social Security tax allowance (Table 3)	+	2,448
12. Income protection allowance (Table 4)	+	30,190
13. Employment expense allowance: • Two working parents (Parents' Marital Status is "married" or "unmarried and both parents living together"): 35% of the lesser of the earned incomes, or \$4,000, whichever is less • One-parent families: 35% of earned income, or \$4,000, whichever is less • Two-parent families, one working parent: enter zero	+	4,000
14. TOTAL ALLOWANCES	=	44,174

*STOP HERE (at line 3) if the following are true:

Line 3 is \$27,000 or less **and**

- The parents did not file a Schedule 1 with their IRS Form 1040 or they are not required to file any income tax return **or**
- Anyone included in the parents' household size (as defined on the FAFSA) received benefits during 2020 or 2021 from any of the designated means-tested federal benefit programs **or**
- Either of the parents is a dislocated worker.

If these circumstances are true, the Expected Family Contribution is automatically zero.

AVAILABLE INCOME		
TOTAL INCOME (from line 7)		75,000
TOTAL ALLOWANCES (from line 14)	−	44,174
15. AVAILABLE INCOME (AI) May be a negative number.	=	30,826

PARENTS' CONTRIBUTION FROM ASSETS		
16. Cash, savings, and checking (FAFSA/SAR #88)		5,000
17. Net worth of investments** (FAFSA/SAR #89) If negative, enter zero.	+	21,000
18. Net worth of business and/or investment farm (FAFSA/SAR #90) If negative, enter zero. ---	+	
19. Adjusted net worth of business/farm (Calculate using Table 6.)	+	---
20. Net worth (sum of lines 16, 17, and 19)	=	26,000
21. Education savings and asset protection allowance (Table 7)	−	3,500
22. Discretionary net worth (line 20 minus line 21)	=	22,500
23. Asset conversion rate	×	.12
24. CONTRIBUTION FROM ASSETS If negative, enter zero.	=	2,700

PARENTS' CONTRIBUTION		
AVAILABLE INCOME (AI) (from line 15)		30,826
CONTRIBUTION FROM ASSETS (from line 24)	+	2,700
25. Adjusted available income (AAI) May be a negative number.	=	33,526
26. Total parents' contribution from AAI (Calculate using Table 8.) If negative, enter zero.		8,820
27. Number in college in 2022–2023 (Exclude parents.) (FAFSA/SAR #73)	÷	1
28. PARENTS' CONTRIBUTION (standard contribution for nine-month enrollment)*** If negative, enter zero.	=	8,820

**Do *not* include the family's home.

***To calculate the parents' contribution for other than nine-month enrollment, see page 11.

Continued on the next page.

REGULAR WORKSHEET Page 2 **A**

STUDENT'S INCOME IN 2020		
29. Adjusted gross income (FAFSA/SAR #36) If negative, enter zero.		3,500
30. Income earned from work (FAFSA/SAR #38)		3,500
31. Taxable income (If tax filer, enter the amount from line 29 above. If non-tax filer, enter the amount from line 30.)		3,500
32. Total untaxed income and benefits (total of FAFSA/SAR #44a through 44i)	+	2,000
33. Taxable and untaxed income (sum of line 31 and line 32)	=	5,500
34. Total additional financial information (total of FAFSA/SAR #43a through 43f)	–	0
35. TOTAL INCOME (line 33 minus line 34) May be a negative number.	=	5,500

ALLOWANCES AGAINST STUDENT INCOME		
36. 2020 U.S. income tax paid (FAFSA/SAR #37) (tax filers only) If negative, enter zero.		0
37. State and other tax allowance (Table 2) If negative, enter zero.	+	165
38. Social Security tax allowance (Table 3)	+	268
39. Income protection allowance	+	7,040
40. Allowance for parents' negative Adjusted available income (If line 25 is negative, enter line 25 as a positive number in line 40. If line 25 is zero or positive, enter zero in line 40.)	+	
41. TOTAL ALLOWANCES	=	7,473

STUDENT'S CONTRIBUTION FROM INCOME		
TOTAL INCOME (from line 35)		5,500
TOTAL ALLOWANCES (from line 41)	–	7,473
42. Available income (AI)	=	(1,973)
43. Assessment of AI	×	.50
44. STUDENT'S CONTRIBUTION FROM AI If negative, enter zero.	=	0

STUDENT'S CONTRIBUTION FROM ASSETS		
45. Cash, savings, and checking (FAFSA/SAR #40)		800
46. Net worth of investments* (FAFSA/SAR #41) If negative, enter zero	+	10,000
47. Net worth of business and/or investment farm (FAFSA/SAR #42) If negative, enter zero.	+	---
48. Net worth (sum of lines 45 through 47)	=	10,800
49. Assessment rate	×	.20
50. STUDENT'S CONTRIBUTION FROM ASSETS	=	2,160

EXPECTED FAMILY CONTRIBUTION		
PARENTS' CONTRIBUTION (from line 28)		8,820
STUDENT'S CONTRIBUTION FROM AI (from line 44)	+	0
STUDENT'S CONTRIBUTION FROM ASSETS (from line 50)	+	2,160
51. EXPECTED FAMILY CONTRIBUTION (standard contribution for nine-month enrollment)** If negative, enter zero.	=	10,980

*Do *not* include the student's home.

**To calculate the EFC for other than nine-month enrollment, see the next page.

D

Six Important Facts About How the EFC Is Calculated

1. Parents and students EACH have a contribution to the EFC based on different assessments of their incomes and assets:

   Parent Contribution:

   4% - 26% parent adjusted gross income
   PLUS
   2.6% - 5.6% parent assets
   (after a small asset protection allowance based on older parent's age)

   Student Contribution:

   50% of student taxed and untaxed income over a fixed income protection allowance of $7,040/year
   PLUS
   20% of student assets (no asset protection allowance)

2. Parents have only one contribution to the EFC no matter how many of their children are in college in a given year. Parent contribution is split among their children attending college that year, which reduces each child's EFC, making them eligible for more need-based aid.
3. The income reported (both student and parent, taxed and untaxed) is from prior-prior year—i.e., if the student is entering college in fall of 2022, the income reported is from 2020.
4. The net value of both parent and student assets is reported *as of the day you* file the FAFSA. See Appendix B for a list of all FAFSA reportable and excluded assets.
5. Student income includes untaxed cash gifts and bills paid on the student's behalf by anyone other than the custodial parents.
6. The EFC formula does not take into consideration your cost of living (except for a very small allowance based on the state in which you live), your consumer debt, any previously acquired college debt, mortgage payments, or other debt.

Four Factors That Can Have a Large Impact on the Size of Your EFC

1. **Parent Income**

   Parent income usually has the biggest impact on the EFC. The table below gives you a rough idea of the effect of parent income on the size of the EFC.

Effect of Parent Income on EFC		
TOTAL PARENT INCOME	% OF PARENT INCOME	CONTRIBUTION TO EFC FROM PARENT INCOME
$25,000	0	-$750
$50,000	4.5%	$2,200
$75,000	10.4%	$7,800
$100,000	16.4%	$16,400
$125,000	19.5%	$24,400
$150,000	21.5%	$32,200
$175,000	22.9%	$40,000
$200,000	23.9%	$47,800
$225,000	24.6%	$55,300
$250,000	25.2%	$62,900
$275,000	25.6%	$70,500
$300,000	26.0%	$78,000
Calculations do not include parent assets or student income and assets and are based on a family of 4 (2 parents, 2 children), living in Ohio, both parents working, equal parent salaries, one child attending college		

© 2021 College Admissions HQ

2. **The Number of Children Enrolled at the Same Time**

   Because the parent contribution to the EFC is split among the children attending college, having more than one child in college at the same time can significantly reduce the EFC for each child (in addition to making each child eligible for more need-based aid).

3. **Student Income Above the Annual Income Protection Allowance**

   After subtracting some tax allowances, 50% of any student taxed or untaxed income above the student income protection allowance of $7,040 is added to the EFC. Many families don't realize that untaxed student income includes cash gifts to a student and any money received or paid on the student's behalf by anyone other than the custodial parents. See Appendix B for a full list of FAFSA reportable and excluded untaxed student income.

4. **Student Assets**

   20% of student assets (savings and checking balances, savings bonds, other investments--see Appendix B for a full list of reportable and excluded student assets) are added to the EFC with *no asset protection allowance*. For example, a $10,000 savings bond in the student's name will raise the EFC by $2,000.

GOOD TO KNOW

Wages earned in college through the Federal Work-Study program are not included in the FAFSA's calculation of your EFC.

It's worth noting that any cash in the student's checking or savings account will be assessed as an asset—even if it is unspent income. For example, every $1,000 of taxed or untaxed income *under* the protection allowance that is unspent the day you file the FAFSA will raise your EFC by $200. And, every $1,000 of taxed or untaxed income *over* the protection allowance that is unspent the day you file the FAFSA will raise your EFC by $700 because it will be assessed twice--as income at 50% and an asset at 20%.

Other EFC Facts

1. Dependent students whose parents have a combined 2020 adjusted gross income of $27,000 or less have an automatic EFC of ZERO as long as one of the following is true:

   a. Anyone included in the parents' household size received federal means-tested assistance during 2020 or 2021 (Medicaid, Supplemental Security Income, SNAP, the Free and Reduced-Price School Lunch Program, TANF, and WIC)

   b. The student and/or parents:

      - filed a 2020 IRS Form 1040, but not a Schedule 1 (unless the Schedule 1 was filed to report: unemployment compensation, an Alaska Permanent Fund dividend, educator expenses, IRA deduction, or a student loan interest deduction), or
      - filed a tax form from a Trust Territory, or
      - were not required to file any income tax return

   c. The student's parent is a dislocated worker

2. Dependent students whose parents have a combined 2020 adjusted gross income of less than $50,000 qualify for the simplified EFC formula (which excludes assets from the EFC analysis) as long as one of the following is true:

   a. anyone included in the parents' household size received federal means-tested assistance during 2020 or 2021 (Medicaid, Supplemental Security Income, SNAP, the Free and Reduced-Price School Lunch Program, TANF, and WIC)

   b. the student's parents:

      - filed a 2020 IRS Form 1040, but not a Schedule 1 (unless the Schedule 1 was filed to report: unemployment compensation, an Alaska Permanent Fund dividend, educator expenses, IRA deduction, or a student loan interest deduction), or
      - filed a tax form from a Trust Territory, or
      - were not required to file any income tax return

   c. the student's parent is a dislocated worker

If I Calculate That My EFC Is Very High, Should I Still File a FAFSA?

Yes!

1. You must file a FAFSA to access Federal Direct Loans, even if you have no financial need.
2. Your EFC might be high enough to disqualify you from need-based aid at many public colleges and universities, but that might not be true at more expensive private schools. You must file a FAFSA to access any need-based financial aid.
3. You must file a FAFSA to access parent PLUS loans, even if you have no financial need.
4. You must file a FAFSA to access many college-awarded scholarship programs.
5. If your financial situation changes for the worse during the school year, the college can adjust your need-based award more easily if you have filed a FAFSA by their deadline.

With an understanding of how your EFC is calculated, you can take steps to keep it as small as possible, as explained in Chapter 4. The lower your EFC the better because you almost always have to pay your full EFC. And, the lower your EFC, the more need-based aid you may get.

2022–2023 EFC FORMULA A: DEPENDENT STUDENT

REGULAR WORKSHEET Page 1 **A**

PARENTS' INCOME IN 2020		
1. Parents' adjusted gross income (FAFSA/SAR #84) If negative, enter zero.		
2. a. Parent 1 (father/mother/stepparent) income earned from work (FAFSA/SAR #86)	________	
2. b. Parent 2 (father/mother/stepparent) income earned from work (FAFSA/SAR #87)	+ ________	
Total parents' income earned from work	=	
3. Taxable income (If tax filers, enter the amount from line 1 above. If non-tax filers, enter the amount from line 2.)*		
4. Total untaxed income and benefits: (total of FAFSA/SAR #92a through 92h)	+	
5. Taxable and untaxed income (sum of line 3 and line 4)	=	
6. Total additional financial information (total of FAFSA/SAR #91a through 91f)	–	
7. TOTAL INCOME (line 5 minus line 6) May be a negative number.	=	

ALLOWANCES AGAINST PARENTS' INCOME		
8. 2020 U.S. income tax paid (FAFSA/SAR #85) (tax filers only) If negative, enter zero.		
9. State and other tax allowance (Table 1) If negative, enter zero.	+	
10. Parent 1 (father/mother/stepparent) Social Security tax allowance (Table 3)	+	
11. Parent 2 (father/mother/stepparent) Social Security tax allowance (Table 3)	+	
12. Income protection allowance (Table 4)	+	
13. Employment expense allowance: • Two working parents (Parents' Marital Status is "married" or "unmarried and both parents living together"): 35% of the lesser of the earned incomes, or $4,000, whichever is less • One-parent families: 35% of earned income, or $4,000, whichever is less • Two-parent families, one working parent: enter zero	+	
14. TOTAL ALLOWANCES	=	

*STOP HERE (at line 3) if the following are true:

Line 3 is $27,000 or less **and**

- The parents did not file a Schedule 1 with their IRS Form 1040 or they are not required to file any income tax return **or**
- Anyone included in the parents' household size (as defined on the FAFSA) received benefits during 2020 or 2021 from any of the designated means-tested federal benefit programs **or**
- Either of the parents is a dislocated worker.

If these circumstances are true, the Expected Family Contribution is automatically zero.

AVAILABLE INCOME		
TOTAL INCOME (from line 7)		
TOTAL ALLOWANCES (from line 14)	–	
15. AVAILABLE INCOME (AI) May be a negative number.	=	

PARENTS' CONTRIBUTION FROM ASSETS			
16. Cash, savings, and checking (FAFSA/SAR #88)			
17. Net worth of investments** (FAFSA/SAR #89) If negative, enter zero.	+		
18. Net worth of business and/or investment farm (FAFSA/SAR #90) If negative, enter zero.	+		
19. Adjusted net worth of business/farm (Calculate using Table 6.)	+		
20. Net worth (sum of lines 16, 17, and 19)	=		
21. Education savings and asset protection allowance (Table 7)	–		
22. Discretionary net worth (line 20 minus line 21)	=		
23. Asset conversion rate	×		.12
24. CONTRIBUTION FROM ASSETS If negative, enter zero.	=		

PARENTS' CONTRIBUTION		
AVAILABLE INCOME (AI) (from line 15)		
CONTRIBUTION FROM ASSETS (from line 24)	+	
25. Adjusted available income (AAI) May be a negative number.	=	
26. Total parents' contribution from AAI (Calculate using Table 8.) If negative, enter zero.		
27. Number in college in 2022–2023 (Exclude parents.) (FAFSA/SAR #73)	÷	
28. PARENTS' CONTRIBUTION (standard contribution for nine-month enrollment)*** If negative, enter zero.	=	

**Do *not* include the family's home.

***To calculate the parents' contribution for other than nine-month enrollment, see page 11.

Continued on the next page.

REGULAR WORKSHEET Page 2 **A**

STUDENT'S INCOME IN 2020		
29. Adjusted gross income (FAFSA/SAR #36) If negative, enter zero.		
30. Income earned from work (FAFSA/SAR #38)		
31. Taxable income (If tax filer, enter the amount from line 29 above. If non-tax filer, enter the amount from line 30.)		
32. Total untaxed income and benefits (total of FAFSA/SAR #44a through 44i)	+	
33. Taxable and untaxed income (sum of line 31 and line 32)	=	
34. Total additional financial information (total of FAFSA/SAR #43a through 43f)	−	
35. TOTAL INCOME (line 33 minus line 34) May be a negative number.	=	

ALLOWANCES AGAINST STUDENT INCOME		
36. 2020 U.S. income tax paid (FAFSA/SAR #37) (tax filers only) If negative, enter zero.		
37. State and other tax allowance (Table 2) If negative, enter zero.	+	
38. Social Security tax allowance (Table 3)	+	
39. Income protection allowance	+	**7,040**
40. Allowance for parents' negative Adjusted available income (If line 25 is negative, enter line 25 as a positive number in line 40. If line 25 is zero or positive, enter zero in line 40.)	+	
41. TOTAL ALLOWANCES	=	

STUDENT'S CONTRIBUTION FROM INCOME		
TOTAL INCOME (from line 35)		
TOTAL ALLOWANCES (from line 41)	−	
42. Available income (AI)	=	
43. Assessment of AI	×	**.50**
44. STUDENT'S CONTRIBUTION FROM AI If negative, enter zero.	=	

STUDENT'S CONTRIBUTION FROM ASSETS		
45. Cash, savings, and checking (FAFSA/SAR #40)		
46. Net worth of investments* (FAFSA/SAR #41) If negative, enter zero	+	
47. Net worth of business and/or investment farm (FAFSA/SAR #42) If negative, enter zero.	+	
48. Net worth (sum of lines 45 through 47)	=	
49. Assessment rate	×	**.20**
50. STUDENT'S CONTRIBUTION FROM ASSETS	=	

EXPECTED FAMILY CONTRIBUTION		
PARENTS' CONTRIBUTION (from line 28)		
STUDENT'S CONTRIBUTION FROM AI (from line 44)	+	
STUDENT'S CONTRIBUTION FROM ASSETS (from line 50)	+	
51. EXPECTED FAMILY CONTRIBUTION (standard contribution for nine-month enrollment)** If negative, enter zero.	=	

*Do *not* include the student's home.

**To calculate the EFC for other than nine-month enrollment, see the next page.

Table 1: State and Other Tax Allowance

EFC Formula A (parents only) – To calculate the state and other tax allowance (line 9), multiply the parents' total income (line 7) by the appropriate percentage from the table below. Use the parents' state of legal residence (FAFSA/SAR #69). If this item is blank or invalid, use the student's state of legal residence (FAFSA/SAR #18). If both items are blank or invalid, use the state in the student's mailing address (FAFSA/SAR #6). If all three items are blank or invalid, use the percentage for a blank or invalid state below.

State	Total Income is $0-$14,999*	Total Income is $15,000 or more*	State	Total Income is $0-$14,999*	Total Income is $15,000 or more*
Alabama	3%	2%	Montana	5%	4%
Alaska	2%	1%	Nebraska	5%	4%
American Samoa	2%	1%	Nevada	3%	2%
Arizona	4%	3%	New Hampshire	4%	3%
Arkansas	4%	3%	New Jersey	9%	8%
California	9%	8%	New Mexico	3%	2%
Canada and Canadian Provinces	2%	1%	New York	10%	9%
Colorado	4%	3%	North Carolina	5%	4%
Connecticut	9%	8%	North Dakota	2%	1%
Delaware	5%	4%	Northern Mariana Islands	2%	1%
District of Columbia	7%	6%	Ohio	5%	4%
Federated States of Micronesia	2%	1%	Oklahoma	3%	2%
Florida	3%	2%	Oregon	7%	6%
Georgia	5%	4%	Palau	2%	1%
Guam	2%	1%	Pennsylvania	5%	4%
Hawaii	5%	4%	Puerto Rico	2%	1%
Idaho	5%	4%	Rhode Island	6%	5%
Illinois	6%	5%	South Carolina	4%	3%
Indiana	4%	3%	South Dakota	2%	1%
Iowa	5%	4%	Tennessee	2%	1%
Kansas	4%	3%	Texas	3%	2%
Kentucky	5%	4%	Utah	5%	4%
Louisiana	3%	2%	Vermont	6%	5%
Maine	6%	5%	Virgin Islands	2%	1%
Marshall Islands	2%	1%	Virginia	6%	5%
Maryland	8%	7%	Washington	3%	2%
Massachusetts	7%	6%	West Virginia	3%	2%
Mexico	2%	1%	Wisconsin	6%	5%
Michigan	5%	4%	Wyoming	2%	1%
Minnesota	7%	6%	Blank or Invalid State	2%	1%
Mississippi	3%	2%	Other	2%	1%
Missouri	5%	4%			

* Percent of Total Income – The percentage varies according to the state and if the total income is below $15,000 or is $15,000 or more

The EFC Formula, 2022–2023

Table 2: State and Other Tax Allowance

EFC Formula A (student only) – To calculate the state and other tax allowance (line 37), multiply the student's total income (line 35) by the appropriate percentage from the table below. Use the student's state of legal residence (FAFSA/SAR #18). If this item is blank or invalid, use the student's mailing address (FAFSA/SAR #6). If both items are blank or invalid, use the parents's state of legal residence (FAFSA/SAR #69). If all three items are blank or invalid, use the percentage for a blank or invalid state below.

State	Percent	State	Percent
Alabama	2%	Montana	3%
Alaska	0%	Nebraska	3%
American Samoa	1%	Nevada	1%
Arizona	2%	New Hampshire	1%
Arkansas	3%	New Jersey	5%
California	6%	New Mexico	2%
Canada and Canadian Provinces	1%	New York	7%
Colorado	3%	North Carolina	3%
Connecticut	5%	North Dakota	1%
Delaware	3%	Northern Mariana Islands	1%
District of Columbia	6%	Ohio	3%
Federated States of Micronesia	1%	Oklahoma	2%
Florida	1%	Oregon	5%
Georgia	4%	Palau	1%
Guam	1%	Pennsylvania	3%
Hawaii	4%	Puerto Rico	1%
Idaho	4%	Rhode Island	4%
Illinois	3%	South Carolina	3%
Indiana	3%	South Dakota	1%
Iowa	3%	Tennessee	1%
Kansas	3%	Texas	1%
Kentucky	4%	Utah	4%
Louisiana	2%	Vermont	3%
Maine	3%	Virgin Islands	1%
Marshall Islands	1%	Virginia	4%
Maryland	6%	Washington	1%
Massachusetts	4%	West Virginia	3%
Mexico	1%	Wisconsin	4%
Michigan	3%	Wyoming	1%
Minnesota	5%	Blank or Invalid State	1%
Mississippi	2%	Other	1%
Missouri	3%		

D

Table 3: Social Security Tax

EFC Formula A – Separately calculate the Social Security tax of parent 1, parent 2, and the student.

- Student's is FAFSA/SAR #38.
- Spouse's is FAFSA/SAR #39.
- Parent 1 (father/mother/stepparent) is FAFSA/SAR #86.
- Parent 2 (father/mother/stepparent) is FAFSA/SAR #87.

Note: The Social Security tax will never be less than zero.

Income Earned from Work	Social Security Tax
$0 – $137,700	7.65% of income
$137,701 to $200,000	$10,534.05 + 1.45% of amount over $137,700
$200,001 or greater	$11,437.40 + 2.35% of amount over $200,000

Table 4: Income Protection Allowance

EFC Formula A

Number in parents' household, including student (FAFSA/SAR #72)	Number of college students in the household (FAFSA/SAR #73)				
	1	2	3	4	5
2	$19,630	$16,270	not applicable	not applicable	not applicable
3	$24,440	$21,100	$17,740	not applicable	not applicable
4	$30,190	$26,830	$23,490	$20,130	not applicable
5	$35,620	$32,260	$28,920	$25,560	$22,220
6	$41,670	$38,310	$34,970	$31,610	$28,270

Note: For each additional household member, add $4,700.
For each additional college student (except parents), subtract $3,340.

Table 6: Business/Farm Net Worth Adjustment

EFC Formulas A (parents only)

If the net worth of a business or farm is—	Then the adjusted net worth is—
Less than $1	$0
$1 to $140,000	40% of net worth of business/farm
$140,001 to $420,000	$56,000 + 50% of net worth over $140,000
$420,001 to $700,000	$196,000 + 60% of net worth over $420,000
$700,001 or more	$364,000 + 100% of net worth over $700,000

Table 7: Education Savings and Asset Protection Allowance

EFC Formula A (parents only)

- Determine the age of the older parent listed in FAFSA/SAR #63 and #67 as of 12/31/2022. If no parent date of birth is provided, use age 45.
- Use the allowance for two parents when the parents' marital status listed in FAFSA/SAR #58 is "Married or remarried" or "Unmarried and both legal parents living together."

Age as of 12/31/2022	*Allowance for two parents or married student*	*Allowance for one parent or unmarried student*	*Age as of 12/31/2022*	*Allowance for two parents or married student*	*Allowance for one parent or unmarried student*
25 or less	$0	$0	46	$3,600	$0
26	200	0	47	3,700	0
27	400	0	48	3,700	0
28	600	0	49	3,800	0
29	800	0	50	3,900	0
30	1,000	0	51	4,000	0
31	1,200	0	52	4,100	0
32	1,400	0	53	4,200	0
33	1,700	0	54	4,400	0
34	1,900	0	55	4,500	0
35	2,100	0	56	4,600	0
36	2,300	0	57	4,700	0
37	2,500	0	58	4,900	0
38	2,700	0	59	5,000	0
39	2,900	0	60	5,100	0
40	3,100	0	61	5,300	0
41	3,200	0	62	5,400	0
42	3,200	0	63	5,600	0
43	3,300	0	64	5,800	0
44	3,400	0	65 or older	5,900	0
45	3,500	0			

Table 8: Contribution from AAI

EFC Formula A – Parents' Contribution from AAI

If the AAI is —	Then the contribution from AAI is—
Less than -$3,409	-$750
$-3,409 to $17,500	22% of AAI
$17,501 to $22,000	$3,850 + 25% of AAI over $17,500
$22,001 to $26,500	$4,975 + 29% of AAI over $22,000
$26,501 to $31,000	$6,280 + 34% of AAI over $26,500
$31,001 to $35,500	$7,810 + 40% of AAI over $31,000
$35,501 or more	$9,610 + 47% of AAI over $35,500

GUIDE TO FINANCIAL AID WHEN PARENTS ARE DIVORCED, SEPARATED, UNMARRIED, OR REMARRIED

- Student Status
- Which Parent(s) Must Report Financial Information on the FAFSA?
- Parents
- Divorce
- The Role of the Financial Aid Officer
- Other Living Circumstances That May Affect Financial Aid
- Reporting Income and Assets on Financial Aid Forms
- The CSS Profile

College financial aid is difficult enough to navigate, but it's even murkier when parents are divorced, separated, unmarried, or remarried. An increasing number of families who are in one of these situations often pay more for college because they don't understand how the rules apply to them.

SEE CHAPTER EIGHT

The following rules apply to the 2022-23 school year. However, many of them will change when the FAFSA changes over the 2023-24 and 2024-25 school years.

Student Status

All students seeking college financial aid are required to report their income and asset information on the FAFSA. And, unless you are an independent student, the FAFSA also requires income and asset information from your parent(s) (either biological or legally adoptive).

To be considered independent for financial aid purposes you must be at least one of the following:

- 24 years old or older
- Married (or separated but not divorced)
- A graduate or professional student
- Providing more than half the financial support for your child(ren) or other dependents
- At any time since age 13, an orphan, in foster care, or a ward of the court
- In legal guardianship or an emancipated minor
- Homeless or self-supporting and at risk for homelessness
- Currently serving in the Armed Forces or a veteran of the Armed Forces

Most students entering college do not qualify as independent and are required to report their parents' financial information.

Which Parent(s) Must Report Financial Information on the FAFSA?

Parent status as married, divorced, separated, unmarried, or remarried affects which parent's information is required in the FAFSA. However, FAFSA definitions of marriage, divorce, and separation are not the same as legal definitions. Which parent should report financial information on the FAFSA becomes clearer when you look at living arrangements.

	Parents' Living Arrangements	Information Required (Biological or adoptive parents)
Married, Unmarried, Separated, Divorced	Living in the same household	Both parents must provide financial information
Married, Unmarried, Separated, Divorced	Living in separate households *(Different floors of the same house or temporary housing such as a hotel room do not count as separate residences)*	The CUSTODIAL PARENT+ must provide financial information (see more information below)
Custodial Parent is Remarried	Parent and step-parent living in the same household	The CUSTODIAL PARENT and the step-parent must provide financial information (see more information below)

+The FAFSA defines "Custodial Parent" as the one with whom the student spends the most time during the year—not the one that claims the student as a dependent for income tax purposes.

Legal guardians, foster parents, grandparents, widowed step-parents, or other relatives, do not have to provide financial information unless they have legally adopted the student.

© 2021 College Admissions HQ

Parents

The Custodial Parent

The "Custodial Parent" for FAFSA purposes is not the same as the parent who has legal custody. The custodial parent is the one the child has lived with the most during the previous 12 months. If the number of days and nights with each parent is equal or the divorce occurred less than a year ago, the custodial parent is the parent who provided more financial support during the previous 12 months. (*Financial support includes child support payments, but also money paid toward food, clothing, housing, medical and dental care, car payments, educational expenses, etc.)*

Choosing the parent with the lower income for the parental financial section on the FAFSA creates the best chance of qualifying for maximum financial aid. But the student needs to live with that parent at least one more day of the year or receive slightly more financial support from that parent to list them as their custodial parent.

SEE CHAPTER EIGHT

The parent who is required to report income and assets will change when the FAFSA changes.

The Step-Parent

The income of a step-parent married to the custodial parent must be reported on the FAFSA, regardless of any prenuptial agreements to the contrary, or unwillingness of the step-parent to help pay for the student's education.

If the custodial parent is remarried as of the date the FAFSA is filed, the student should answer questions about both the parent and step-parent, in the same way you would report a biological or adoptive parent living in the same household. This is true even if the marriage hadn't occurred during the year for which income is considered (prior-prior year). For example, if the custodial parent married in 2021 before the student files the 2022-23 FAFSA, the step-parent must still report their 2020 income.

If the custodial parent dies, the step-parent's information is no longer reported on the FAFSA (unless the step-parent has legally adopted the student) even if the student continues to live with the step-parent. In this situation, financial support provided to the student must be reported as untaxed student income on the FAFSA unless the support is part of a legal child support agreement.

If the step-parent's financial information is required on a FAFSA for his or her legal child, and the step-parent provides more than half the support for his or her step-child, regardless of where the step-child resides, the step-parent may count the child and step-child as part of their household size on the FAFSA.

Students Living with Neither Parent

If a student lives with someone who has not *legally adopted* them (legal guardians, foster parents, grandparents, widowed step-parents, or other relatives), the adults' financial information (including Foster Care payments) is not reported on the FAFSA.

However, cash support provided to the student or paid on the student's behalf must be reported as untaxed student income on the FAFSA. This includes monetary gifts and money paid for housing, food, clothing, car payments, medical and dental care, and college costs.

GOOD TO KNOW

20% of any untaxed student income above the student annual income protection allowance of $7,040 is added directly to the EFC. See Chapter 3 and Appendix D for an explanation of how a family's EFC is calculated.

SEE CHAPTER EIGHT

Most untaxed student income will no longer be reported when the FAFSA changes.

Death of a Parent

If the custodial parent dies, the non-custodial parent's financial information must be reported on the FAFSA. If the student has no meaningful contact with and receives no support from the non-custodial parent, the college's financial aid administrator may make an exception to this rule.

If no legal parent (biological or adoptive) remains, the student is considered independent on the FAFSA.

If a surviving parent dies after the FAFSA has been filed, the student must update her dependency status and report income and assets as an independent student.

Which Parent Gets the Income Tax Benefits?

The parent who claims the child as a dependent may be eligible to take advantage of qualified education tax deductions and credits, whether or not he or she is the custodial parent.

Divorce

Newly Divorced

If a student's parents filed a joint return for the tax year applicable to the current FAFSA but have since separated, divorced, remarried, or been widowed, only the custodial parent's information should be reported on the FAFSA. The student must also submit an IRS tax transcript and W-2 for the custodial parent and speak with the college's financial aid administrator to be sure any misinformation is corrected.

(This is the same procedure for an independent student who has recently separated, divorced, or been widowed.)

Planning to Divorce

It is widely advised that parents planning to divorce should spell out the burdens of college costs for each child individually in their divorce settlements. In states where this is required, if the parents cannot reach an agreement, the court will decide.

Consider carefully:

- Where the money will come from to pay for college (529s, savings, home equity, income, education loans, etc.)
- What are acceptable expenses (tuition, room, board, transportation, supplies, study abroad, club fees, health insurance, etc.)
- Who is responsible for which expenses
- How many semesters of support are acceptable (many students now take up to six years to complete their 4-year degree)
- What happens in the event of a gap year or the child does not attend or finish college
- Child support payments through college graduation
- Age limits on college attendance
- Requirements the child must satisfy to receive continued support (such as a minimum GPA, or credit hours)
- Restrictions on which colleges the student may attend
- Is the money paid directly to the college or to the student
- Who will take on, co-sign, and/or pay back private student loans

The Role of the Financial Aid Officer

The college's financial aid officer has the final word on how much financial aid a student will receive. Many colleges use their own formulas to award financial aid and may require an Institutional form in addition to the FAFSA (but usually not in addition to the CSS Profile).

Even when they require financial information from both parents (and step-parents), they may still take a divorce into account in their financial aid calculations by factoring in the costs of living in separate households.

In cases where it cannot be determined who qualifies as the custodial parent, the college financial aid administrator will decide which parent is responsible for completing the FAFSA–usually the parent with the greater income.

Other Living Circumstances That May Affect Financial Aid

Common-Law Marriage

If a couple meets the criteria in their state for a common-law marriage, they should be reported as married on the FAFSA.

If the state does not consider their situation to be a common-law marriage, they are not considered married on the FAFSA, and a dependent student would follow the rules for divorce to determine which parent's information to report.

Domestic Partners

If a parent is living with, but not married to another person, the non-parent's information should not be reported on the FAFSA.

A Parent Who Isn't Willing to Comply

Call the financial aid office to ask about their specific policies under these circumstances. Sometimes colleges will make an exception to what is required if it can be shown that the non-compliant parent has a history of non-support.

Reporting Income and Assets on Financial Aid Forms

How to Report Alimony and Child Support

Alimony received by the custodial parent is considered taxable parent income and would be included on the FAFSA as such. There's no need to report it again separately. Child support is reported on the FAFSA as untaxed parent income.

How to Report a 529

- 529 Accounts Owned by the Custodial Parent
  - Reported as a parent asset on the FAFSA
  - Distributions are not reported as student income on the FAFSA
- 529 Accounts Owned by the Non-custodial Parent
  - Does not get reported as an asset on the FAFSA
  - Distributions are reported as student income on the FAFSA
- The CSS Profile will require information about 529 accounts owned by both parents (and grandparents)

SEE CHAPTER EIGHT

Child Support will be assessed as a parent asset instead of income, and distributions from a 529 account that does not belong to the reporting parent will no longer be reported as untaxed student when the FAFSA changes.

The CSS Profile

In addition to the FAFSA, about 240 colleges, universities, and scholarship programs, usually the most generous ones, require that students file the CSS Profile, a much more exhaustive look at family finances that usually requires extensive financial information from both parents and often that of step-parents. Depending on the larger family financial picture, it may be a financial aid advantage or disadvantage in applying to schools that require the CSS Profile. Appendix C is a complete guide to the CSS Profile.

E

FINANCIAL AID GLOSSARY

Frequently Encountered Acronyms

COA (Cost of Attendance) The "sticker price" of a college which represents the sum of direct expenses (tuition, fees, room, and board) and indirect expenses (the average cost of textbooks, supplies, and personal spending).

EFC (Expected Family Contribution) A number generated by the FAFSA's assessment of parent and student income and assets that represents the dollar amount a family is expected to pay toward the cost of college each year. Unless the student is awarded merit aid that exceeds his or her need, the EFC is the minimum the family will pay. The EFC is recalculated each year the student applies for financial aid. The EFC is used by the federal and state governments and the colleges to determine eligibility for need-based financial aid, including grants, loans, and Work-Study.

FAFSA (Free Application for Federal Student Aid) A government form that analyzes parent and student income and assets to generate a family's EFC (see above), which is used to determine eligibility for federal, state, and college grants, federal and state loans, and Work-Study.

FSA ID (Federal Student Aid ID) An identification made up of a username and password required for all students and parents of dependent students filing a FAFSA. The FSA ID allows you to fill out, amend, and sign your FAFSA online and provides access to the National Student Loan Database to keep track of your federal student loans over the life of those loans.

PLUS Loan (Parent Loan for Undergraduate Students) Federal fixed-rate education loans, up to the full COA (minus grants and scholarships awarded), available to parents without an adverse credit history.

SAI (Student Aid Index) A number generated by an assessment of parent and student income and assets on the FAFSA. The SAI will replace the EFC in either 2023-24 or 2024-25, depending on how quickly the Department of Education can fully implement the changes in the FAFSA Simplification Act. Like the EFC, the SAI will represent the minimum dollar amount a family is expected to pay toward the cost of college. The SAI will be used by the federal and state governments and the colleges to determine eligibility for need-based financial aid, including grants, loans, and Work-Study.

SAR (Student Aid Report) A report sent to the colleges and the student after he or she files the FAFSA. The SAR contains all the information entered into the FAFSA and is used to help the college determine the student's eligibility for financial aid.

529 Investment Plan A tax-advantaged investment savings plan authorized by Section 529 of the Internal Revenue Code meant to be used for future college expenses and/or K-12 private school tuition. Account holders may establish an account for themselves or a beneficiary and use the money to pay for tuition, room and board, mandatory fees, required books, and computers.

529 Pre-Paid Plan A tax-advantaged savings plan that buys future tuition credits at eligible colleges and universities at current prices.

Academic Rigor The level of intensity of the coursework at a college, including number of classroom hours, expected study hours per week, level of student collaboration, level of faculty interaction with students, writing requirements, and student presentation expectations.

Acceptance Rate The percentage of students accepted from the applicant pool.

Accrued Interest The accumulated interest on the borrowed amount of a student loan that has not yet been paid.

Admissions Tests College entrance exams that help college admissions officers compare applicants by providing a standardized way to evaluate their readiness for college level work. The main college admissions tests are the SAT, ACT, and SAT Subject tests.

Approximate Cost A rough estimate of what a given college will cost you using a net price calculator. Your actual net price may be different depending on scholarships and/or grants the college may award you.

Asset Protection Allowance A dollar amount of parent assets, based on the age of the older parent, that is not included when determining the family's EFC.

Award Letter The official notice from a college of the type and amount of financial aid being offered to an accepted applicant, including grants, scholarships, loans, and Work-Study.

Borrower The person legally responsible for repaying a loan who has signed and agreed to the terms and conditions of the loan.

Bursar's Office The college department responsible for the billing and collection of the school's charges.

Capitalized Interest Interest that is due, but not paid, that is added to the loan principal. Capitalizing interest increases the size of the loan, which results in greater interest charges, and, therefore, increases the total cost of the loan.

Class Rank Compares academic achievement between students in the same grade in high school through evaluation of both the difficulty of the classes taken and the grades earned.

CLEP (College-Level Examination Program) Tests Standardized tests not connected to a specific high school course that measure knowledge of subjects at the college level and may be accepted by colleges for awarding college credit.

Co-Signer A credit-worthy individual, usually a parent, who agrees to share the responsibility for student loan repayment with the borrower.

COA (Cost of Attendance) The "sticker price" of a college which represents the sum of direct expenses (tuition, fees, room, and board) and indirect expenses (the average cost of textbooks, supplies, and personal spending).

College Credit Full course credit awarded to students for successful completion of college courses taken in a college or a high school dual enrollment program, or for a specific AP or CLEP score.

College Navigator A college search engine and database of statistical information of over 7,000 institutions run by the federal government's National Center for Education Statistics.

Common Data Set A standardized form into which colleges can choose to enter specific data about their admissions statistics, enrollment and persistence statistics, academic programs, expenses, financial aid statistics, and other institutional information.

Consolidation Loan A single loan that pays off multiple other loans and brings their balances together into one payment, often with more favorable terms.

Coverdell Education Savings Account (ESA) A tax-advantaged savings plan for the qualified education expenses of a named beneficiary, such as a child or grandchild. Qualified education expenses include college costs (tuition, fees, room, board, books, and supplies) and certain elementary and secondary school expenses.

CSS Profile (College Scholarship Service Profile) A highly thorough financial aid form required, usually in addition to the FAFSA, by approximately 240 colleges and universities and some scholarship programs. The CSS Profile costs money to submit.

Default Failure to repay a loan in accordance with the terms of the agreement or promissory note.

Deferment The temporary postponement of loan payments during which interest may or may not be charged and accrued, depending upon the type of loan.

Delinquency Incidents of late or missed loan payments, as specified in the terms of the promissory note or agreement.

Dependent Student A student who is financially dependent upon a parent or legal guardian or does not meet the criteria for being classified as an Independent student. A student is considered Dependent for the purpose of financial aid *unless* he or she is over the age of 24, in a graduate program, married, supporting a child, an orphan, an emancipated minor, a foster child, homeless, or in the armed services.

Direct Costs The portion of tuition, fees, room, and board costs at a college that you are responsible for paying. Direct costs appear on your bill.

Direct Student Loans Low-interest, fixed-rate federal education loans available to all students who file the FAFSA, regardless of need, to help pay the cost of college.

Disbursement The act of paying out the funds borrowed from a loan.

Discharge The release of borrowers from their obligation to repay their loans.

Discount The process by which a college offsets its published sticker price with grants and/or scholarships to entice students (usually those without financial need or special merit) to attend.

Discretionary Income For the purposes of college loan repayment calculations, the amount of money by which adjusted gross income exceeds the poverty line.

Education Loans Federal Direct Student loans, Federal Parent PLUS loans, state student loans, and private student loans (offered by banks, credit unions, and other lending institutions) used to pay the costs of attending college.

EFC (Expected Family Contribution) A number generated by the FAFSA that represents the dollar amount a family is expected to pay toward the cost of college each year. Unless the student is awarded merit aid that exceeds his or her need, the EFC is the minimum the family will pay. The EFC is determined by an analysis of the family's income and assets and is recalculated each year the student applies for financial aid. The EFC is used by the federal and state governments and the colleges to determine eligibility for need-based financial aid, including grants, loans, and Work-Study.

EFC Formula Guide A free online government form that includes information about the formula used to generate the EFC. Included worksheets allow users to accurately calculate their family's EFC and understand what impacts the size of their EFC.

Employer Tuition Assistance An employer-sponsored benefit offered by some employers to help employees and/or their dependents pay the costs associated with higher education.

Endowment Money and other assets donated to a college by alumni, the community, and other patrons. The endowment is invested in order to generate income to help run the college's yearly operations.

Exit Counseling A group, individual, or online session during which borrowers who are leaving school or dropping below half-time enrollment receive information about their student loan repayment obligations and update their contact information.

Extended Repayment Plan A Direct Loan repayment option that allows borrowers to take up to 25 years to repay the balance. Payments may be fixed or graduated.

FAFSA (Free Application for Federal Student Aid) A government form that analyzes parent and student income and assets to generate a family's EFC (see above), which is used to determine eligibility for federal, state, and college grants, federal and state loans, and Work-Study.

FAFSA4caster A federal online calculator that generates a rough estimate of your EFC based on data you enter. The FAFSA4caster will be replaced in September 2021 with a new calculator, The Federal Student Aid Estimator.

FAFSA Simplification Act A part of The Consolidated Appropriations Act 2021 signed into law in December of 2020. It calls for key changes to Federal Student Aid, including the FAFSA form, need analysis, Pell Grant eligibility, and many other financial aid policies and procedures. It will affect every school that participates in the Federal Title IV program (student financial aid) and every state that uses FAFSA data to award state aid. Changes will be fully implemented by the 2024-25 school year.

Federal Direct Student Loans Low-interest education loans through the federal government available to all students (regardless of need), issued in the student's name, to help pay the cost of college.

Federal Perkins Loan A federal education loan for students with high need issued through the college in the student's name. The Perkins Loan program was allowed to expire on September 30, 2017. The last disbursements were received June 30, 2018. There is now only one federal student loan, the Federal Direct Student Loan (see above).

Federal PLUS Loan Fixed-rate education loans offered by the federal government to parents without adverse credit histories. Parents can borrow up to the full cost of attendance (minus grants and scholarships).

Federal Student Aid Estimator A federal online calculator that generates a rough estimate of your EFC and your eligibility for federal student aid. The Federal Student Aid Estimator replaced the FAFSA4caster in Setember 2021.

Fees Monies charged by the college to each student, either separately or rolled into tuition, to cover certain parts of the college's operations such as campus activities, technology, transportation, facilities, student centers, health centers, and general maintenance, regardless of whether or not students use these services.

Financial Aid Money used to pay the COA including federal, state, and/or college grants; federal, college, and/or outside scholarships; Federal Direct Student loans; state loans, and Work-Study.

Financial Aid Award An aid package consisting of grants, scholarships, education loans, and/or Work-Study arranged through the college to help pay the cost of attendance at a given college.

Financial Aid Award Comparison A comparison of the Net Price you will pay at colleges that have accepted you.

Financial Aid Office The college or university office responsible for awarding financial aid and providing financial aid counseling.

Financial Need The difference between the school's Cost of Attendance (COA) and the student's Expected Family Contribution (EFC).

Fixed Interest Rate A rate of interest that does not change during the life of the loan.

Forbearance An arrangement to postpone or reduce a borrower's monthly payment amount for a limited and specified period, during which interest is charged and accrued.

Four-Year Graduation Rate The percentage of students who graduate in four years from the same college or university at which they started.

FSA ID (Federal Student Aid ID) An identification made up of a username and password used by students and parents of dependent students filing a FAFSA online. While not required, the FSA ID is the fastest way to sign the FAFSA and have it processed and is the only way to access or correct information online, or to pre-fill a FAFSA with information from your previous year's FAFSA. The FSA ID also provides access to the National Student Loan Database System (NSLDS) to keep track of your federal student loans over the life of those loans.

FSEOG (Federal Supplemental Educational Opportunity Grants) Need-based grants available through participating colleges using federal money and awarded to students with exceptional financial need.

Full-Time Student A student who carries an academic workload that is considered full-time, as determined by the school, usually 12 credit hours per semester.

Gap The dollar amount of unmet need in a financial aid package (Need = COA – EFC). Need is first met with any scholarship money you have been awarded, whether from the college itself or an outside organization. Next, federal and state grants (if you are eligible), Federal Direct Student loans, state loans, and Work-Study are applied. If there is any remaining need, the college will offer its own need-based grant aid in accordance with its own financial aid policies. Most college grants do not cover all of the remaining need, leaving a Gap that the family is responsible for paying in addition to their EFC, Federal Direct Student loans, and Work-Study.

Gap Year A year between high school graduation and entering college during which a student chooses a different activity such as language immersion, wilderness experiences, internships, volunteer work, travel, or a job.

Gift Aid Free money that does not have to be paid back, including grants (based on need and awarded by federal and state governments and/or the college itself) and scholarships (based on merit and awarded by the college or an outside organization).

Grace Period A six to nine month period before the first payment must be made on a student loan. The grace period starts the day after a borrower ceases to be enrolled at least half time.

Graduated Repayment Plan A Direct Loan repayment plan that allows monthly payment amounts to start out small and gradually increase every two years during the repayment period.

Grant Money from the federal and state governments and/or the college itself that does not have to be paid back.

Federal Grants Pell & FSEOG, awarded to a student based on financial Need as determined by the FAFSA. TEACH, awarded to students in certain education programs. IASG, awarded to certain military families.

State Grants Grants usually reserved for student residents attending in-state colleges or students whose states have reciprocity agreements with other states.

College Grants Grants awarded by the college based on the college's financial aid policies and the student's Need (as determined by the FAFSA and/or the CSS Profile and Institutional financial aid forms).

Half-Time Student A student who carries an academic workload that is considered at least one-half the workload of a full-time student, as determined by the school.

High School Profile A document created by your high school that outlines the school's academic practices, the scope of the core classes, the numbers of AP and Honors classes offered, the average standardized test scores (SAT, ACT, AP) of the senior class, an explanation of the grading and ranking system, the graduation rate, the number of seniors who go on to college, and a list of colleges they attend.

IASG (Iraq/Afghanistan Service Grant) Grants for students whose parents died as a result of military service performed in Iraq or Afghanistan after 9/11/2001. A student does not have to establish need to receive an IASG award but does have to file a FAFSA. The IASG award is always equal to that year's Maximum Pell Grant. If an IASG-qualifying student also qualifies for a Federal Pell Grant, eligibility for the Pell Grant will be recalculated as if their Expected Family Contribution (EFC) were zero and they will receive the Maximum Pell Grant. A student cannot get both the IASG and a Pell Grant.

Income-Based Repayment Plan (IBR) A Direct Loan repayment option that caps monthly payments based on income and family size, and forgives remaining debt and interest after 25 years.

Income Contingent Repayment Plan A Direct Loan repayment option that allows the monthly payment amounts to vary with the borrower's income, and forgives remaining debt and interest after 25 years.

Income Protection Allowance The amount of income protected within the EFC formula based on the number of people in the parents' household and the number of college students in the parents' household.

Income Share Agreement (ISA) An arrangement between an organization or individual and a student in which some portion of the student's tuition is paid in exchange for a percentage of the student's future income for a fixed number of years.

Independent Student For financial aid purposes, a student who meets one of the following criteria: 24 years old or older, enrolled in a graduate or professional program, married, orphaned, in foster care, homeless, an emancipated minor, a ward of the court, a veteran of or on active duty in the armed services, have legal dependents other than a spouse, or have documents describing unusual circumstances that allow a financial aid officer to make the determination of independence.

Indirect Costs Costs to attend college that do not appear on your college bill, including textbooks, supplies, travel, and personal expenses.

Institutional Needs The internal priorities of a given college that guide their decisions when constructing a freshman class including the need for specific athletes or artists, filling certain majors, students who will increase the socioeconomic, racial, or regional diversity of a given class, or students who can pay all or most of the COA.

Interest A loan expense charged by the lender and paid by the borrower for the use of borrowed money. The expense is calculated as a percentage of the principal amount (loan amount) borrowed.

IRA (Individual Retirement Account) An investment tool used for retirement savings, but which may also be used for qualified higher education expenses.

IRS Data Retrieval Tool (DRT) A method for the direct transfer of your tax information from the IRS to your FAFSA available approximately 1-2 weeks after electronic filing of your taxes and 6-8 weeks after paper filing.

Legacy Applicant A student whose parent(s), sibling(s), or other close relative(s) attended the school to which that student is applying.

LIBOR (London Interbank Offered Rate) An international benchmark for calculating interest rates. Private loans with variable rates may be based on the LIBOR 3-month rate or the LIBOR 1-month rate.

Loan Money borrowed that must be repaid.

Loan Limits The maximum amounts students may obtain through federally funded student financial assistance programs. Loan limits vary by type of loan, academic level, program length, and whether a student is Dependent or Independent.

Loan Principal The total sum of money borrowed.

Loan Servicer The organization responsible for management and billing of a student loan.

Master Promissory Note (MPN) The legal document in which you promise to repay your Federal Loans and accrued interest to the U.S. Department of Education.

Meeting Need is a term that refers to how and to what extent a college awards different kinds of financial aid (federal, state, and college grants; federal and state student loans; Work-Study; college and outside scholarships) to help pay your financial need. Once all federal and state aid you qualify for and any scholarship you are awarded are applied to your need, each college will award a college grant, based on its financial aid policies, to your remaining need. The vast majority of colleges (97%) do not award enough college grant money to meet all your remaining need and leave you with a Gap in financial aid.

Meeting Full Need Colleges that pledge to meet full need will not leave you with a Gap in financial aid. They award enough college grant money to cover the difference between the COA and the family's EFC + Direct Student loans + Work-Study. Only 3% of accredited 4-year colleges and universities in the U.S. pledge to meet full need.

Merit Aid Scholarship money from colleges or outside organizations that does not have to be paid back. Merit aid is awarded to students for their outstanding academic, creative, or athletic talents or achievements.

Need The difference between the cost of attendance (COA) at a school and the family's EFC.

Need-Based Aid Financial aid offered to help cover your financial need. Need-based aid comes in the form of federal, state, and college grants, Federal Direct Student Loans, state education loans, and Work-Study.

Need-Blind Admission The policy of a small number of colleges in the U.S. to make admission decisions without considering the financial circumstances of its applicants.

Net Price The actual amount of money you must pay to attend a college each year, including EFC, Self-Help Aid (government loans and Work-Study), and any Gap (unmet Need).

Net Price Calculator An online calculator, usually found on a college's website, that estimates a student's Net Price at that school.

National Student Loan Data System (NSLDS) The Department of Education's central location for information on federal student loans. With their FSA ID, students can access information on each of their federal loans including the type of loan, college attended when loan was obtained, disbursement date, loan status, loan interest rate, and contact information for the loan servicer.

Origination Fee A fee charged and deducted from the proceeds of a loan before the loan is disbursed.

Out-of-Pocket Costs The college costs the family is responsible for paying right before the school year begins including EFC + Work-Study + Gap (unmet Need).

Pell Grant Federal need-based aid given to students with EFCs below ~$5,850. Students must file a FASFA on time to access Pell grants and, if eligible, are guaranteed to get the amount of Pell Grant they qualify for each year. The size of your Pell Grant is dependent on your financial Need as determined by the FAFSA. Maximum award for 2021-22 is $6,495.

Personal Expenses Costs the student incurs while at college not related to academics or room and board, including extra food, toiletries, transportation, laundry, and entertainment.

PLUS (Parent Loan for Undergraduate Students) Federal fixed-rate education loans, up to the full COA (minus grants and scholarships awarded), available to parents without an adverse credit history.

Prepayment Any payment on a loan by the borrower before it is required to be paid under the terms of the promissory note.

Principal The amount of money borrowed by the student before interest has been charged.

Priority Date The due date for college applications in order to be given the strongest consideration for admission, housing, and financial aid.

Private Education Loans Loans used to pay all or part of the COA, in the student's name usually with a credit-worthy co-signer, issued through banks, credit unions, or other lending institutions that set fixed or variable interest rates based on credit scores.

Promissory Note A legally binding contract between a lender and a borrower containing the terms and conditions of the loan.

Public Service Loan Forgiveness A program for federal student loan borrowers that forgives remaining debt, tax-free, for people who work in nonprofit, government, and public service jobs after 10 years of qualifying payments.

Rehabilitation Loans A new loan created after 12 consecutive payments have been made on a formerly defaulted loan, and the borrower again becomes eligible for participation in federal financial aid programs.

Repayment Disclosure The notice sent from your loan servicer during your grace period that provides you with loan details such as the principle balance, the projected amount of interest you will pay, your first payment due date, and the amount of your monthly payments.

Repayment Period The period of time a borrower is responsible for repaying his or her loans.

Repayment Schedule A statement provided to the borrower that lists the total amount borrowed, the amount of monthly payments, and the date payments are due.

SAR (Student Aid Report) A report sent to the colleges and the student after he or she files the FAFSA. The SAR contains all the information entered into the FAFSA and is used to help the college determine the student's eligibility for financial aid.

Scholarship Gift Aid awarded to a student for exceptional academic, artistic, or athletic ability to help pay college expenses that comes from the college itself or an outside organization and does not have to be paid back.

Self-Help Aid Financial aid consisting of Federal Direct Student Loans, state education loans (if available), and federal Work-Study.

Six-year Graduation Rate The percentage of students who graduate in six years from the same college in which they started.

Standard Repayment Plan The default repayment schedule that calculates student loan payments over a 10-year period.

Sticker Price The cost of attendance (COA) at a given college, including the sum of direct expenses (tuition, fees, room, and board) and indirect expenses (the average cost of textbooks, supplies, and personal spending).

Subsidized Direct Student Loan A federal loan for students with need in which the federal government pays the interest while borrowers are enrolled at least half-time, during the six-month grace period following graduation, and during authorized periods of deferment.

TEACH Grants (Teacher Education Assistance for College and Higher Education Grants) Federal grants available to students who have applied for the grant, are enrolled as education majors at a school that participates in a TEACH-grant eligible program, and agree to teach for 4 of the 8 years following graduation in a high-need field of education or in an area that services low-income families.

Tuition and Fees The cost of taking classes at a college plus the money charged to each student to help pay for the college's operational costs.

Tuition Payment Plans Interest-free installment plans offered by the college that divide your college bills into equal monthly installments of 10 – 12 months.

UGMA/UTMA (Uniform Gifts to Minors Act/Uniform Transfer to Minors Act) Savings vehicles in which money owned by a minor is held in a custodial trust and managed by an adult, usually the parent or grandparent.

Unsubsidized Direct Student Loan Loans in which interest is charged throughout the life of the loan. The borrower may choose to pay the interest charged on the loan or allow the interest to accrue.

Work-Study A federal program of college-supported, part-time employment for students with financial need.

ABOUT THE AUTHORS

Elizabeth Walter and Debra Thro are American School Counselor Association (ASCA) Certified College Admissions Specialists and members of Pennsylvania Association for College Admission Counseling (PACAC).

Liz and Deb, friends for nearly 20 years, began learning about the college admissions process, college costs, and the college financial aid system through the experiences of their own children and those of their friends. As tenacious researchers and determined optimists who both strongly believe in the power of knowledge, they created College Admissions HQ, a website offering free access to college admissions resources to give families critical information that can truly change students' lives.

As the cost of college has skyrocketed during the last decade and the collective U.S. student loan debt has ballooned to more than $1.6 trillion, Liz and Deb decided to write Pay Less for College to provide parents and students with the tools they need to avoid the college debt burden that has plagued so many families.

Liz holds a PhD in Experimental Pathology from Case Western Reserve University and is a mom of three terrific young adults.

Deb is also a mom of three terrific young adults and holds a BA in Communications and Social Science from the University of South Florida.

ACKNOWLEDGEMENTS

We wish to thank the following people for their advice, support, kindness, and talents: Emily Ray Ryan, Jacob Thro, Dennis Thro, Megan Dimit, Dustin Dimit, Sydney Tucker, Andrew Tucker, Jack Ryan, Nick Ryan, Gabriel Ryan, Lynne Parrish, Kelsie Parrish, Stacy Ryan, and Gayle Baker.